D0646557

Allies of the Earth

Gustav Krollmann, *Mission Range, Montana*. Northern Pacific Railway poster, ca. 1935. Author's collection.

I love planes, but they do sometimes make me feel the world is composed of Boston, Chicago, and Los Angeles tied together loosely by TWA, American, and United. I love cars, but they are simply an amplified version of all the frustrations and confrontations of everyday life. Buses I have never liked.

On a train, however, you get, if you look and can see, a deep, abiding sense of the continuity of the processes of nature and life.

—Georgie Anne Geyer, 1977

Train travel...is a place to contemplate life rather than push against it, the journey a luxury for the spirit as much as for the body. Unlike the dejected bus atmosphere or the cold airplane stratosphere, the train trip inspires conversation, seats single passengers together in the dining car, encourages a mapping of the unexpected.

—Susan Rich, 1999

In the course of [train] trips I have learned to feel the simple truth of time. Not necessarily time for relaxation, but time to observe, to contemplate, to discover portions of this country I had taken for granted or knew nothing about.

—Michael Frome, 1963

Also by Alfred Runte

National Parks: The American Experience

Trains of Discovery: Western Railroads and the National Parks

Yosemite: The Embattled Wilderness

Public Lands, Public Heritage: The National Forest Idea

Praise for *National Parks: The American Experience*

"As for the policy-makers—at Interior, on the Hill, and in the White House—*National Parks* is a must." — *Washington Post Book World*

"Remains the best book on national parks…. Runte generates new understanding of the changing perceptions of environmentalism." — *New Mexico Historical Review*

"Essential reading for the student who has an interest in conserving natural ecosystems." — *Journal of Applied Ecology*

Praise for *Yosemite: The Embattled Wilderness*

"A powerful and important book, a critical contribution to Yosemite historiography and ideology at a time when the politicizing of the National Park Service and the vast hordes of visitors pose genuine threats…to the natural environment of Yosemite." — *Western American Literature*

"This analysis is applicable to every park, wilderness, and national treasure; it is a warning for every conservationist to be on guard against the pressures for development." — *Naturalist Review*

"His work is alive, and even more than his fine research and clear writing, his passion accounts for the wide readership he enjoys." — *Environmental History Review*

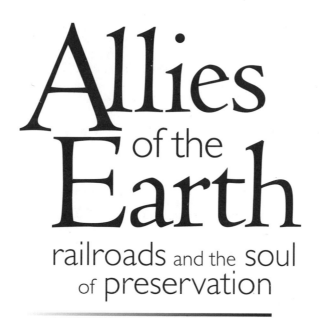

Allies
of the
Earth

railroads and the soul
of preservation

Alfred Runte

TRUMAN STATE UNIVERSITY PRESS

Published by Truman State University Press, Kirksville, Missouri
tsup.truman.edu

Cover painting, *Spirit of the Water Gap* © 2005 by J. Craig Thorpe. Oil on canvas, 24 x 16 inches. Commissioned by Charles and Mary Jo Mott specifically for the cover of *Allies of the Earth: Railroads and the Soul of Preservation*. Used by permission of the artist.

Historical photography by Nancy Hines, University of Washington.

Cover design: Teresa Wheeler

Type: Text is LegacySerITC—copyright URW; display is Optima—copyright Linotype Library GmbH or its affiliated Linotype-Hell companies.
Printed by: Thomson-Shore, Dexter, Michigan USA

Library of Congress Cataloging-in-Publication Data

Runte, Alfred, 1947–.
    Allies of the earth : railroads and the soul of preservation / by Alfred Runte.
       p. cm.
    Includes bibliographical and index references.
    ISBN-13: 978-1-931112-52-9 (hardcover : alk. paper)
    ISBN-10: 1-931112-52-5 (hardcover : alk. paper)
    1. Railroads—United States—History. 2. Railroads—United States—Passenger traffic. I. Title.
    TF23.R85 2006
    385'.0973—dc22
                                               2005016920

For dear mentors across the years and miles—
Walter E. Smith, Michael Frome, Carsten Lien, and Ben W. Twight

And always for my artist and visionary—J. Craig Thorpe

Contents

Illustrations

Preface

We Americans have been without good railroads so long we have virtually forgotten what railroads do—do for people, that is, not just for commerce. Above all, railroads encourage us to respect the land. Once it would have been unthinkable that Americans would abandon a technology so complementary of natural beauty, but we did abandon it. This book will explore that cultural disconnect in a manner consistent with our forgetfulness: What did we have? Why did we lose it? And how do we get it back?

That we should want it back may seem counterintuitive, and yet we cannot deny our history. Above and beyond our obsession with the economy, the land is our identity. With the decline of the passenger train we lost the struggle to make beauty part of our daily lives. Increasingly, our most beautiful landscapes are remote, defined principally by wilderness and the national parks. Even there, the forgotten story is the railroads, whose promotion of parks greatly assisted preservationists. Suddenly, the railroads stopped caring—stopped beckoning to anyone, even if the caring had been just promotion. More to the point, Americans stopped believing the railroads should care. Why should corporations have a social conscience? Let the railroads obsess about the economy too.

This book will define why America, through its railroads, should insist on the partnership we let go. Neither the railroads nor we can escape the advantages of that partnership, beginning with construction that values art. Railroad architecture delights us still, from the stone masonry of Starrucca Viaduct to the cavernous interior of Grand Central Terminal. Each special gateway promised a right-of-way that was itself a work of art. This is why preservationists believed in railroads. For the railroad companies, publicizing the land may have been economic, but it helped preservation too. From the start, railroad design was imbued with a genuine sensitivity for all that a passenger sees from a train. A railroad remains what it is—a statement about the land, not mindless conquest.

This much is certain with the decline of railroad travel: we have ceased reveling in ourselves as a continent. The creation of Amtrak in 1971 only hardened the nation's growing perception that beauty and size

The dining car of the *Lake Cities,* late winter 1967. The photographer and his friends have just arrived for breakfast, expectantly waiting their passage through the Delaware Water Gap. Photograph courtesy of Walter E. Smith.

were obstacles. Consider a passenger train doing 80 mph—still doing only 80 mph. How in the 1970s could that be "progress?" Agreed, America should keep a few trains for commuting and perhaps, when they really could go *fast,* reconsider trains for longer distances. Otherwise, take one from coast to coast? What possessed anyone still to be thinking *that*?

No wonder we have forgotten landscape, having fixated on speed for all these years. Speed can be wonderful; Europe proves that and Japan's bullet trains have proved it too. Finally, even American trains, mostly in the Northeast, are winning back passengers solely through faster schedules. But what does faster mean for landscape—speed at any cost? Why deny, just for the sake of efficiency, what originally led us to believe in the passenger train as so much more?

To be sure, distances in America are greater than in Europe, and population densities lesser (for now), but is that not the point? America still has something worth discovering; the West is awesome space. East or west, conceding that growth is here to stay is not the same as conceding that it need be ugly. America once believed (as Europe still believes) in trains as the servants of public space. Europe knows to use railroads for preservation, while America forgets what it truly wants preserved.

Ironically, it was during the so-called environmental decade of the 1960s that the decision to drop trains was finalized. What markets might the railroads have protected where the passenger train still excelled? The government was funding interstate highways; where might government have lent the railroads equivalent aid?

Cars and airplanes were not inevitable—they were the nation's choices. Allowing itself a limited mandate, apparently the nation felt that two out of three modes was good enough. But we may choose to assess technology rather than accept it blindly. Imagine returning the country to a balance. Imagine a country served by a reasonable minimum of passenger trains, everywhere, one in the morning, afternoon, and night. For once, invite the possibility that we made the wrong choice, or at least that our choices have been incomplete.

Even as America came to believe in the environment, it somehow missed preserving that earlier belief in landscape. Making a wiser choice for travel is not about making our worst habits greener. Although we dared not see this when trains were commonplace, let us dare to see it now. The passenger train, as a means of movement and preservation, is still the choice too good to lose.

No book is an individual enterprise, no matter who gets to write it. Forty years ago, a dear friend, Walter Smith, started me down the path of railroad history. Together we crisscrossed the cradle of American railroading in Maryland, New York, and Pennsylvania, Walt endlessly describing the influences of geography and natural resources on rail development. Above all, he challenged me to consider how railroads had been a way of life. Sensing the twilight of our hometown railroad (and his employer, the Erie-Lackawanna), he also determined that my lessons should come first-hand. I got used to phone calls in the middle of the night, Walt suggesting we wake our girlfriends and take the train to New York City. "My God, Walt, it's 3:00 AM!" I had all my life to sleep, he reminded me, but the trains would soon be gone. How could I say no? So an hour later the four of us would be stumbling aboard the *Lake Cities* in Binghamton, New

York, hoping to squeeze in a few more winks. Even if our excitement had allowed that, there was always the steward's pleasant wake-up call. *Bong, bing, bong!*—his mallet lightly hit the keys of a little xylophone. "Breakfast is now being served. Dining car to your rear."

It was indeed our favorite ritual, descending the Pocono Mountains in the dining car. At the midpoint of our journey, the sky had brightened and the scenery came to life. Filing in, we took our seats beside the window, marveling at the tablecloth and heavy silver. Of course, beginning with coffee was a must; we loved the burnished pot, its scratches hinting at many stories. "Try the corn muffins next," Walt always insisted, noting they were made on board from scratch. Once a deer sprang from the forest and paced us briefly beside the tracks, then darted back into the underbrush as we too sped on our way. "A buck!" Walt said, "Look at the antlers on that thing!" He added that the dining car made all such sightings special.

Finally, the forest would break into openings, the trees framing a river off to our left. "Delaware Water Gap," Walt delighted in announcing as together we slouched in our seats to see the cliffs. Within minutes, the waiter appeared balancing a tray, setting down our eggs and hash browns with a flourish. "Be right back with your toast and bacon, folks." "Not to hurry," Walt reassured him. "We have everything we need." Walt understood the changes coming to railroads; he knew that we needed less sleep and more of such good memories. We needed, later when our breakfasting eyes fell on parking lots, to remember this river and this train.

In recent years, another colleague, J. Craig Thorpe, picked up where Walt left off. Craig reminds me that what people find inspiring, they celebrate in art. The art of the railroads inspired Americans to believe in a greater good. In that spirit, Craig offered me a cover painting and line drawings showing the relevance of trains today. He is right—his art will clarify whether we believe the changes in these landscapes to be wise or just expedient.

Other friends, some of them railroad workers, have also taken me into their confidence. Years ago Dan Monaghan and the late Charlie Luna steered me through the maze of railroad economics. The late Edward Ullman, a professional geographer, inspired me by example and, like Charlie Luna, served with distinction on the Amtrak board. Arthur Lloyd and the late Ralph Kerchum made every trip to San Francisco a lesson in railroad history. When Kerchum was invited to join the Amtrak board, Lloyd continued supporting him from the wings, as did Bruce Heard, another Amtrak veteran with years of commitment to public service. Certainly, the trains of America were never better served by such dedicated individuals and their associates.

I hold similar admiration for Ron Scheck, Michael Frome, Carlos Schwantes, Keith Bryant, Al Richmond, Don Hofsommer, Don Phillips, Bill Withuhn, Richard Orsi, Gordon Chappell, Gordon Gill, and the late Robin Winks. As curators, cultural historians, journalists, and professors, all have explored, with appropriate criticism, the subject of railroads in American life. Similarly, Chuck Mott, Lloyd Flem, Tony Trifiletti, and Hal Cooper of the Washington Association of Railroad Passengers personify the dedication of countless national activists, all giving generously of their time and treasure to advance railroads culturally and politically. George Thompson and Randall Jones of the Center for American Places guided this project in its early stages and delighted when I found a publisher as committed to it as they were.

Over the years, I have been indebted to the staffs of many federal, state, and local historical sites and museums. For this volume, the archives of Steamtown National Historical Site proved of special significance. Admittedly, Steamtown's location in Scranton, Pennsylvania, tells only part of the railroad story. However, my theme being landscape, I believe Steamtown's role to be exceptional—there is no finer example of a railroad's commitment to place than Scranton's historic Lackawanna Station. Park Historian Patrick McKnight generously provided images and reports of the station's tiled landscape panels. As evidence of railroad art, their renown is grandly duplicated by Tunkhannock and Starrucca Viaducts, built in the nearby mountains north of Scranton. Combining art and engineering, these bridges add to Steamtown's indisputable importance as a national repository of railroad history. That Steamtown National Historical Site cannot possibly cover every theme only proves the need for additional museums and historical sites.

Granted, Steamtown does represent my past. This is the railroad landscape I came to know while traveling from Binghamton on the Lackawanna Railroad. Regardless, any historian would find this a proper place to start a study of railroad landscapes. The cradle of American railroading is the East, and the Lackawanna Valley was among the first places railroad artists painted.

To name all the others who have helped me with this project would read like a checklist of IOUs, so I will resist and simply say thank you. And of course, I thank Christine, who gladly married trains along with me. Her enthusiasm makes special those trips of discovery where each of us knows not to fly or drive. Surely life, like a good train, is better when sharing the window with someone you love.

The Earth on Display

It was 1915, the place was San Francisco, and America's railroads were stealing the show. The nation (and an estimated 18 million visitors) believed the focus of the huge celebration underway at the Panama–Pacific International Exposition was the completion of the Panama Canal. But the railroads were packing the house with their message: they were the proud owners of America the Beautiful. In the Palace of Transportation at the exhibit called "The Globe," four railroads had bypassed the Panama Canal entirely, presenting the transcontinental railroad in miniature. "The earth itself is on display," they announced. "The United States, with its mountains, rivers, valleys, national parks, and cities, is taken in at a glance. In fact, the eye travels with tiny trains which flit across the huge miniature exactly as the trains they represent are in flight across the continent." Even if the Panama Canal became important, the railroads held the land and had since 1869. The cities glowing in the exhibit were their achievement and so too were the national parks. "Yellowstone, Mesa Verde, Rocky Mountain, and Yosemite National Parks and Great Salt Lake are indicated by squares of soft light." No canal would be taking that business from the railroads. America the Beautiful was theirs to sell.[1]

Indeed, all the railroads had come to the fair to advertise, sparing no expense. Hosting the largest exhibit, the Atchison, Topeka & Santa Fe

1

Railway had appropriated six acres for a giant replica of the Grand Canyon. Visitors skirted the rim "in an electric observation parlor car," stopping at "seven of the grandest and most distinctive points." More than 100 miles of the canyon were on display, "reproduced accurately, carefully and wrought so wonderfully that it is hard to realize that you are not actually on the rim of the Canyon itself." Not to be outdone, the Union Pacific Railroad was exhibiting Yellowstone on four acres, including "the Great Falls of the Yellowstone," its "grandeur akin to the original." Dominating the grounds filled with other "natural wonders," a full-size replica of the Old Faithful Inn seated two thousand for lunch and dinner. "There is no curtailment in proportions," the railroad reported, "no elimination of details. The reproduction is exact." Patrons dined while enjoying an eighty-piece orchestra, then stepped outside to watch a replica of Old Faithful Geyser steaming to full height "at regular intervals, uniform with those of its prototype."[2]

And the railroads were just getting started. On the roof of the Grand Canyon diorama, a Pueblo Indian Village, inhabited by Pueblo Indians, displayed their life and art. And members of the Blackfeet tribe in full ceremonial dress greeted visitors entering the Great Northern Railway building, promising "a wonderful display of the beauties of Glacier National Park." The even grander building of the Southern Pacific Railroad featured "the Glade, where are reproduced with most natural effect in beautiful landscape settings noted scenes on Southern Pacific lines." The Glade won the grand prize.[3]

Although the eastern railroads were well represented, it was obvious why the western railroads had spent so lavishly. After all, the show was all about the continent, and the West represented the American dream. In the mind's eye, the Panama Canal was not about heading east. As if that message might be lost in San Francisco, San Diego dared to repeat it, offering a second exposition, hardly less popular, on the grounds of Balboa Park.

The railroads' exhibits were so memorable they were talked about for decades. In tracing the origins of the National Park Service, its founders acknowledged the importance of 1915. A third major conference on

As a reminder that they had opened the country first, America's railroads participated lavishly in the 1915 California expositions celebrating the completion of the Panama Canal. In this brochure, the Union Pacific describes its exhibits. Author's collection.

Poster stamps were popular among American railroads, inviting passengers to advertise through the mails. On this stamp, Union Pacific features its Yellowstone exhibit at the 1915 Panama–Pacific International Exposition. At $500,000, the display cost two and a half times as much as the original Old Faithful Inn built in 1904. Author's collection.

national parks, hosted by the Interior Department, divided its program between the University of California–Berkeley and the San Francisco exhibit grounds. Delegates met in the Southern Pacific Auditorium. As at the 1911 and 1912 conferences, all of the principal railroads were represented.[4] The next year in Washington DC, their executives again linked arms with preservationists, testifying in Congress in support of a government agency that would carry the spirit of 1915 forward. The resulting agency, the National Park Service, could reasonably credit its creation to the power of the railroads—and to the great expositions where the railroads had opened America's eyes to landscape. Never again would American technology and a love of continental vastness seem as close as they were then. Although the alliance had many proud moments ahead, they somehow lacked the same exuberance. By the 1960s, all of it—the exhibits and the conferences, the testimony on behalf of parks, the belief that natural beauty was best seen from a train—was just a memory.

Few environmentalists today know to acknowledge it, but this is preservation's missing link. Back at "The Globe" in 1915, the exhibit's railroad sponsors continued their effusive praise of the American land. "When the visitor has reached the center of the earth, as it were, the effect is exactly as though one were standing in a garden on a matchless summer night."[5] Think of it. These were the railroads, America's most hardened corporations, talking about believing in natural beauty. At the moment they stopped talking about the earth, preservation lost a timeless ally. Who would not agree, watching the march of asphalt, that we need them to talk that way again?

Following page: The cover of this Union Pacific leaflet (ca. 1960) comparing airplane and train fares has an unmistakable message that railroads better serve the landscape. Note the cloud formation suggesting the famous plume of Old Faithful Geyser. Author's collection.

The Places We Rode

As late as 1929, approximately twenty thousand passenger trains served the 130 million residents of the United States.[1] Of course, the numbers were a bit deceiving, just as they are today. Many trains operated shorter distances, connecting neighboring cities. Like commuting, those trips were considered routine; however, the moment longer distances entered the equation, the character of the passenger train wondrously changed. Then a state or region might be involved, and possibly a journey from coast to coast. Trains going somewhere looked the part. The finest among them, a railroad's so-called varnish, were luxurious beyond compare, each heralded to be the signature of that railroad and its landscape.

A comparable level of service today would still require trains numbering in the thousands. Instead, barely a handful cross the country, and an equally small number go north and south. The rest act like commuter trains, plying the routes between the cities and the suburbs. The popular term today for these routes is corridors, as if train passengers no longer look left or right.

And so less than a century later, we have forgotten that railroads once dominated the environment. For years, the principal selling point of the passenger train was an American sense of place. After all, the passenger train was itself a place, each with its own separate name and identity. Identity today is static; travel is focused more on where we are going and less on how we get there. The passenger train was all about place, and the trains put a community—a place—in motion.

The railroads named each community boldly, preferring major cities and prominent landscapes. Everything betokened place. Then it was still the Pennsylvania Railroad, the Delaware & Hudson, and the Santa Fe. No one would have dreamed of using an acronym like Conrail or CSX. What do those mean anyway? Railroads believed in the opportunity of pacing the country, calling out the names. A passenger train celebrated the changing landscape, even as the train itself stayed the same.

Suddenly, railroads deny it is their responsibility to celebrate anything. America is not so sure. The columnist Georgie Anne Geyer remains one of the eloquent holdouts, defining trains as the flow of life. "Pieces fit together. They overlap. People work together. The dependencies and interdependencies of real life are laid out before you like a perfectly woven shawl. Cities fade into countryside and rain edges into sunlight and the little houses wait for the whistle that tells them it is all together."[2]

Spectators also share the experience, if only to wish they were on board. One moment, a person is alone beside the tracks, and suddenly a whole community comes gliding through. The mind fills in the blanks. Where has this train been? Where is it going? What places will it visit next? Isn't our first reaction to instinctively turn to wave? We might (but rarely do) show the same affection for an airplane or a bus. Nothing comparable, nothing spontaneous, reassures us that buses or planes are special. The modern airplane is sold as a destination, ignoring the magic of reaching out to it. A bus partakes of a right-of-way we might discover for ourselves. Our thrill for a passing train is in the knowledge that we cannot capture what it does anywhere else.

Without trains, the gulf between place and technology in transportation is very wide. No airport or expressway wins public affection the way the railroads did. Even sitting at the gate, an airplane appears somehow inaccessible and aloof. The windows of a plane seem superfluous, as if traveling has nothing to do with place. Hoping to locate a friend or loved one, we can only count backward from the nose; even then, the face squinting through the dinky window probably belongs to someone else.

The wonder of trains in the landscape was a popular subject of railroad calendars. As children wave, the caption announces: "Every season brings its own beauty to the Water Level Route." In 1959, Alfred Hitchcock used similar settings in the Hudson River Valley for his train scenes in *North by Northwest*. Painting signed "Gould" (John Gould). Author's collection.

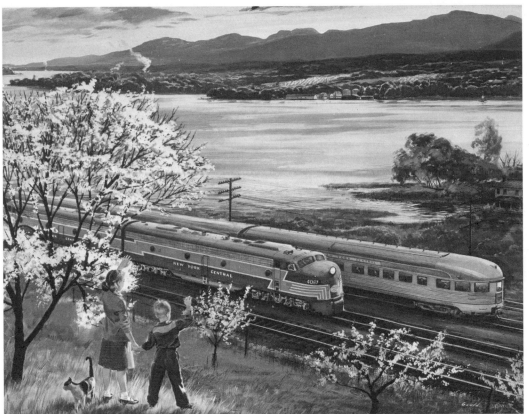

Every season brings its own beauty to the Water Level Route

NEW YORK CENTRAL SYSTEM

FIRST MONTH	JANUARY 1954					FIRST MONTH
SUN	**MON**	**TUE**	**WED**	**THU**	**FRI**	**SAT**
● NEW MOON 4th	◗ FIRST QUAR. 11th	○ FULL MOON 18th	◖ LAST QUAR. 26th		**1** NEW YEAR'S DAY	**2**
3	**4**	**5**	**6**	**7**	**8**	**9**
10	**11**	**12**	**13**	**14**	**15**	**16**
17	**18**	**19**	**20**	**21**	**22**	**23**
24 **31**	**25**	**26**	**27**	**28**	**29**	**30**

DECEMBER 1953							FEBRUARY 1954						
SUN	MON	TUE	WED	THU	FRI	SAT	SUN	MON	TUE	WED	THU	FRI	SAT
		1	2	3	4	5		1	2	3	4	5	6
6	7	8	9	10	11	12	7	8	9	10	11	12	13
13	14	15	16	17	18	19	14	15	16	17	18	19	20
20	21	22	23	24	25	26	21	22	23	24	25	26	27
27	28	29	30	31			28						

THE SMOOTH, SCENIC WATER LEVEL ROUTE

14947 SANTA FE TRAIN IN CROZIER CANYON, ARIZONA.   FRED HARVEY.

This Fred Harvey postcard (ca. 1910) celebrates Arizona's lovely Crozier Canyon, recently destroyed by mining for ornamental rocks. The protective influences of American railroading are now missing from the national landscape. Author's collection.

We can never be sure. Most buses have generous windows but seating and aisles no wider than an airplane's. Missing is a train's sense of reassurance, a conviction that while we are changing places outside, the place we occupy inside is special too.

Airplanes offer utility—yes, we will get there fast. Otherwise, place is defined as the row where the passenger sits, not what the passenger sees. Life moves in one direction—squeezed together and facing front. On a train, we can reverse the seats and face one another; we are free in an instant to move about. We may venture to another coach, often a lounge car or a diner. Most long-distance trains maintain their observation cars, sometimes even the traditional domes that made them famous. On a train, if someone is bothersome or distracting, we have many options for finding another seat. Conversely, those same options allow us to invite newfound friends into our lives.

Aboard an airplane, where you sit is where you stay. If clouds cooperate, the window overlooks a relief map; otherwise, landscape is only a distant option. Either that or someone decides to pull the shades the moment you are airborne. In the past, pilots offered at least some familiarity with the largest sights below; now, any commentary would disrupt the movie. If the landscape is still your personal choice, you are hopelessly singled out, the light spilling through your window announcing your reluctance to conform. The interior of an airplane is all about conformity, and always will be so.

In contrast, a train cannot possibly be on the way to somewhere by denying the worth of where it is. Every city, farm, and village still comes with faces and countless waves. Our waves and smiles return the compliment; windows mean exchange. A train will always have two destinations, the moment being lived and the one to come.

Without denigrating the speed of an airplane, speed is all it has to offer. Security dictates how to board, higher altitudes dictate the smaller windows. The moment after takeoff, all associations with landscape and community fall away. The airport itself cowers behind security fences with even more security measures in between. Speed comes at a price. The greater the risk of failure (perhaps even the threat of sabotage), the less an airline can trust its passengers, and worse yet, the less we trust one another. Loss of trust is the price of airplanes as surely as the opposite is the wealth of trains.

Granted, railroads began as conquerors, both of people and the landscape. Labor was expendable and, good grief, think of the federal government's generosity! Think of the western land grants totaling an area approximating the size of California, Oregon, and Washington state.[3] The railroads intended those lands for sale and settlement—for the conquering hand of fields and farms. No railroad tycoon bemoaned the death knell of the bison or native cultures—all that is true enough. But lost in the tragedy of what the railroads changed is the level of responsibility they did accept. At least the railroads believed in saving something; with highways, even the smallest thing saved has been an afterthought.

Railroads, by suggesting something immutable, lent a focus to development. Although railroad companies were developers and tourism is about promotion, the way to keep the tourists coming was to offer them the landscape undefiled.

Heading west, tourists from the East or Midwest would be in transit for several days, crossing the faces of many landscapes. Building the promise of a destination called for building patience along the way. In this vein, Clive Irving, a British journalist, believes that American culture has collapsed. "Americans have tragically deserted the most heroic element of their own continent: size," he writes. "With many other Europeans, I feel that Americans are strangers to their own country in a way that no European can be." The reason, Irving argues, "is the demise of the American railroad."[4]

It was after all European explorers and European artists who first felt the magic of the continent. The conviction that travel could be inspirational impressed Europeans as the distinguishing theme of the American passenger train. "One cannot denigrate the expedience of America's domestic airline network, a true wonder of the world," Irving admits, "but neither should one enlist it as the agent of the ultimate travel experience." A sense of captivation, indeed of belonging, is still with those who stay "earthbound."[5]

Irving's conviction is all the more sobering because the railroads once provided that experience. Now having abandoned the railroads, few Americans see the relationship. The threat of terrorism has not dissuaded us; our principal instructors regarding the meaning of distance remain the airlines. To the airlines, distance is an obstacle—something the traveler endures and overcomes.

If technology limited the railroads (or coerced them), they nonetheless respected the limitation by preserving what the passenger might hope to see. A frivolous disregard for landscape was not among their faults. Rather, they thought just the opposite—landscape attracted passengers. As early as 1858, the Baltimore & Ohio Railroad prepared a special train for artists and photographers (studio and darkroom included), all to capture, for public consumption, the boldness of eastern scenery. Harpers Ferry, Virginia (one year later the site of John Brown's raid), merited a special stop, as did the Tray Run Viaduct over the Cheat River Gorge. In 1859 *Harper's New Monthly Magazine* enthusiastically reported about the trip, noting that "the beautiful scenery" had inspired the hoped-for paintings and photographs. Thanks to the railroad, those landscapes had finally been made "known to the general public." Then came John Brown and the Civil War, and temporarily the railroad's dreams were stayed.[6]

A 1927 Northern Pacific brochure, *2000 Miles of Startling Beauty!* (page 45), invites westbound travelers to count the mountain ranges. During construction, the railroads were mindful that frivolously destroying the national landscape would compromise their ability to promote destinations. Author's collection.

Montana Rockies

Count the Mountains!

SEE all the Northern Pacific mountains you can on your journey, for they are unsurpassed anywhere in the world!

Twenty-eight ranges are visible from your train window—the same vast mountains that Lewis and Clark overcame, rich now in the lore of pioneer days in the Northwest, wearing the mantle of glamor that gold prospector, railroad builder, and "dude" rancher have put upon their mighty shoulders!

This is the "March of the Mountains" as it appears to the watchful westbound Northern Pacific traveler:

Wolf Range—South of Hysham, Montana.
Beartooth Range—Southwest of Billings.
Bridger Range—Bozeman to Belgrade, north.
Gallatin Range—Livingston to Bozeman, south.
Absaroka Range—South of Livingston.
Crazy Mountains—Reed Point to Mission, north.
Madison Range—Bozeman to Three Forks, southwest.
Tobacco Root Range—Sappington to Whitehall, south.
London Hills Range—Seen from Sappington, north.
Gravelly Range—Whitehall to Homestake, south.
Ruby Range—Whitehall to Homestake, southwest.
Snowcrest Range—West of Whitehall.
Continental Divide—Main Range of the Rockies, Whitehall to Silver Bow.
Blue Mountains—Whitehall to Pipestone Springs, north.
Highland Mountains—Seen from Butte, south.
Continental Divide—Seen from Helena and vicinity.
Big Belt Range—North of Townsend, Winston and Helena.
Elkhorn Range—Toston to Helena, south.
Anaconda Range—Butte to Garrison, west.
Flint Creek Range—Deer Lodge to Gold Creek, north.
Deer Lodge Mountains—Same as Flint Creek Range.
Garnet Range—Drummond to Bonner, north.
Sapphire Range—Drummond to Missoula, south.
Mission Range—Arlee to McDonald, northeast.
Bitter Root Range—Missoula to Lake Pend Oreille, south.
Coeur d'Alene Mountains—Paradise to Cabinet, southwest.
Cabinet Mountains—Paradise to Heron, north.
Selkirk Range—Oden to Rathdrum, northwest.
Cascade Mountains—Lakeview to Bucoda, east.
Olympics—Coast cities (clear weather).

No matter, the scenery would still be there, and after the war, the scenery rapidly became a favorite selling point for every railroad. Following the lead of artists, railroads promoted the vernacular landscape—in the East, the blending of farms and villages was often described as the pastoral and the picturesque. Because artists might further agree that humans added interest to the landscape, again, what better reason for building railroads? There were artists who disagreed, but rarely when a commission was at stake.[7] Either way, the railroads seemed to be holding back. Notable rivers especially, when paralleled by a railroad, implied that industry might charm the wilderness, animating the landscape simply by following a river's sweeps and curves.

In the West, railroads, following the explorers again, confirmed the magnificence of the "sublime." Here nature, more than simply being beautiful, suggested a sweeping power. Thus the completion in 1869 of the first transcontinental railroad presaged a wealth of opportunities. In California, Yosemite Valley was already a public park, including the Mariposa Grove of giant sequoias. Proclaimed the equivalent of the pyramids, the sequoias delighted railroad publicists. Certainly, tourists would be eager to prove the point (eschewing Egypt) by seeing California for themselves. Next, in 1871, Congress embraced the idea of a public park in Yellowstone. From the wings, the Northern Pacific Railway cheered its approval mightily, then, after the park had been established in 1872, hired still more publicists. Since the railroad's main line was expected to cross Montana Territory only 50 miles to the north, the company correctly anticipated a virtual monopoly over the first groups of geyser-seeking tourists.[8]

The thought of Yellowstone's wonders lying at the end of a railroad journey excited anyone's expectations. But for the journey itself to meet those expectations, the railroad must provide wonders in between. Frederick Billings, as president of the Northern Pacific, urged that no landscape be expendable. Construction, especially up the Yellowstone River Valley, should consider carefully the scenery through which tourists in the future would need to pass. Billings wisely reasoned that no railroad failing those landscapes could hope to sell its wondrous destinations.[9]

Wherever the scenery was less spectacular (in some opinions, at least), a railroad would rely on history, conjuring up images of the colorful characters who had passed that way before. Tourists in the heartland might dream of the explorers, the forty-niners, and the pioneers. They too had found the prairies monotonous and the plains downright daunting in their quest. They too had scanned the horizon, hoping for the first rise of the Rocky Mountains. If railroad tourists would "feel" the history, they might sense the excitement of those landscapes. Not unlike Lewis and

Clark, the railroad traveler was being "initiated." First came the monotony, and then the cathedral-like majesty of the mountainous West.

Whether intentional or cynically materialistic, the railroads' effect on construction was largely positive. Railroads quickly learned to sell their presence as a complementary force for changing the landscape. Granted, the Rocky Mountains were bored with tunnels and their canyons lined with steel. By 1900, tracks twisted beside dozens of rivers, and that did mean cuts and fills. Where there were forests, trees were quickly felled when railroads appeared. At least the railroads were considering landscape and tried not to leave hopeless scars. At least a railroad right-of-way allowed the scenery to recover, if not initially to prevail.

In contrast, permanent scars are the legacy of the automobile, and not just because four-lane highways are so wide. Unlike a railroad, nothing about a highway protects the landscape by limiting development to determined stops. At any time and in any place, a vandal may pull off the road, breaking bottles and painting graffiti across the cliffs.

If a railroad is abandoned, nature instantly goes to work. Ballast and ties are gloriously ripe for vegetation; weeds and brush literally invade. Seeking the former right-of-way of the Delaware & Hudson Railroad in Lanesboro, Pennsylvania, the sharpest eyes can barely make it out or walk it easily, now that sprouting trees are replacing brush. How long before a similar recovery might happen on a superhighway? Just consider the depth and steepness of the cuts. If they are bare rock (and many are), trees can barely hang on—those scars will be around for centuries, reminding future generations (if not present ones) that the singular difference between the railroad and the highway was indeed respecting landscape.

The point is, who believes a big scar could (and should) be a smaller scar when big scars are all they know? Who even sees it as a scar? Thanks to highways, a hill or mountainside stripped to bedrock is all too common now. For railroads there was little need of that, and railroads wished to avoid it even then. Where the route got too steep, the railroads simply tunneled. Cuts and embankments, where needed, similarly benefited the landscape by being narrow. Although these were changes and had a permanence, nature still had a chance. Every spark of conscience among the railroads was magnified by the minimalist needs of construction. They could not help but be stewards, even when they least thought of it.

Hollywood also reminds us what the combination of luck and conscience meant for landscape. In the classic Alfred Hitchcock film *North by Northwest* (1959), we are introduced to a famous train, the *Twentieth Century Limited*.[10] Intended for the business traveler, it was the New York Central's finest, departing from New York City in the early evening, generally around 6:00 PM. By 9:00 AM Central Time (just as its opposite arrived in

New York), the *Century* would arrive in Chicago, having covered 966 miles in sixteen hours.[11]

Hitchcock's hero is a New York advertising executive played by Cary Grant. Framed for murder, he makes his getaway through Grand Central Terminal, the elegant point of departure for the equally elegant *Century*. However, Grant's picture is there ahead of him, and he is recognized at the ticket window. He has no choice but to try the gate. Pleading he has come to see someone off, he manages to rush the agent and slip aboard the waiting train.

Unfortunately, he has no ticket and his pursuers are right behind him. Whereupon fate intervenes—a young woman he met in the corridor (Eva Marie Saint) sends his pursuers in the wrong direction. Grant still must elude the conductors, who will ask for tickets once the train is moving. An open restroom provides a temporary refuge—his luck has held again. A better refuge would be the dining car, where his business suit should convince the staff he is a paying passenger like any other.

Arriving in the dining car, he just happens to find Miss Saint (are we surprised?) with a table to herself. The next scene, building on railroad custom, is Hitchcock at his best. In every dining car across America, passengers know to share their tables. The steward simply must agree which one. Miss Saint will later confess that she tipped the steward to seat Grant at hers. But for now, he has no reason to suspect a thing. Meanwhile, Alfred Hitchcock and the *Twentieth Century Limited* have set the perfect romantic mood—a handsome gentleman, a beautiful woman, and the possibility they are meeting on the train by chance.

Now imagine that scene on an airplane—"Fat chance," we would say. Sure, couples meet on airplanes, but is there the same level of credibility? For one thing, Cary Grant would be in handcuffs by now. And Miss Saint would be fighting for a seat next to him. What passenger would willingly swap? Any hint of romance surviving that argument would hardly endure through the peanuts. Meet strangers on an airplane? Fall in love besides? Not likely. On planes, the principal movement is to the restroom. Where you sit is where you stay.

The Hudson River, perhaps the East's most famous landscape, rewarded travelers with views of the United States Military Academy at West Point and Storm King Mountain. In 1935, passengers hoping to learn more about the river's history and landscape were given this colorful guidebook. Cover painting signed LR (Leslie Ragan). Author's collection.

A similar intimacy with the landscape is also out of the question. Hitchcock carefully picked his couple's diversion (and ours)—the magical Hudson River highlands. The steward has given them a window facing west, which is also the river side. Rising in the distance above the opposite shore, the mountains are a deepening blue. Speckled clouds hint of a brilliant sunset that will paint the waters red. The experience on the screen reflects what the *Century*'s passengers dined with every day.

Today, may not every compromise of the American landscape be linked to what became of such remarkable hosts? Where is the highway that with the same conviction has taught respect for the Hudson Valley? Where is the *Century*'s message of preservation? Dear Traveler: This landscape inspired the Hudson River school of art, founded by the brush of Thomas Cole. In folklore, Rip Van Winkle slept twenty years among these mountains, and Washington Irving wrote the *Legend of Sleepy Hollow* here. There is West Point overlooking the river, and below are the estates of many great national leaders. Dear Traveler: We who manage and run the New York Central Railroad are pleased you came with us.

Today, if we feel more than nostalgia watching this movie, we feel remorse at the loss of the *Century*. Because we deserted the *Century* and all trains like her, these landscapes lost their voice. Perhaps Alfred Hitchcock was telling America that the country was about to do something stupid by throwing that voice away. Is that why, at the end of the scene, the *Century* fades into a silhouette, lost in the darkening river, sky, and mountains? The train's presence is still evincing stewardship, but now we can believe that the scene meant good-bye.

It is in retrospect that regrets grow comparative. A highway, we finally realize, will always ask for more. Trains asked little but to please us, and those we just let go. With them went the subtleties of the American landscape, scenes innocently beautiful and close to home. Our spectacular landscapes we may have. Everywhere else, we fight to preserve what is gentle and serene.

There is perhaps the reason—blunt now—on the screen. We stopped incorporating into our national consciousness the conviction that every landscape is important. Preservation does not end with parks. If we had believed that in time, the *Twentieth Century Limited* might still be teaching us. Then let us dare believe it now. We need trains again as a reminder of how best to move and what not to miss.

The Legacy of *Phoebe Snow*

Most historians agree that the industry most symbolic of the American landscape is the railroad. Granted, the automobile now covers the country, but the railroad built it first. The name Union Pacific still says it elegantly. Not only did it join the country east to west, the railroad also healed the division between North and South. Only so grand a project could have fulfilled Abraham Lincoln's wish that the nation move past the carnage of civil war.

It was Lincoln who, in 1864, affirmed the dream of a national landscape by approving legislation to protect Yosemite Valley and the giant sequoias. The challenge now is to explain why Americans so often forget the relationship and the history—why even environmentalists tend to ignore how railroads protected landscape. Consider a nighttime photograph taken from space. How many of us would see in the lighted sprawl a confirmation of the loss of railroads? East of the Mississippi River, the landscape is ablaze. Meanwhile, in the West, the tentacles of glare are rapidly expanding. In the surviving blackness may lie the American wilderness, but those places too will certainly be lost if the nation does not restore discipline to transportation.

As America fills up its open spaces, the wonderment evoked by the sight of a distant horizon is in jeopardy. The national population in 1946 was barely 150 million—the start of the Baby Boom. Between the Baby

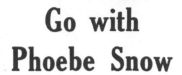

Boom and immigration, there are now 145 million more of us—295 million all told. We drive 230 million motor vehicles. The Census Bureau predicts that by 2050 the population will reach 404 million Americans, with 571 million expected by 2100. Even the first figure is historically sobering. Over the next forty-five years, the nation will be compelled to absorb the equivalent of its total growth in the 300 years between the Pilgrims and the end of World War I.[1]

Increasingly, large parts of the Northeast, Texas, Florida, and California are approaching the population density of Europe and Japan. In that situation, can our current system (let alone our expectations) handle 100 million more Americans relying on cars and airplanes? Can we afford to lose all those farms and forests (another 100 million acres at the current rate of 2.2 million acres per year)?[2] Consider too the added pressure on national parks and wilderness. Is our confidence in that future realistic? Is it possible or reasonable to grow indefinitely, believing our system of transportation does not need to change?

No doubt, the automobile still clouds the issue by accommodating the dreams of the pioneers. Like the covered wagon, the automobile allows us just to pick up and move on. We mentally leapfrog back to a time of pioneer clearings and the headlong rush to change the landscape wholesale. Consequently, even lands saved through public ownership cannot escape feeling like reservations. Outside of those lands, reality intrudes everywhere. Main Street America is being obliterated by fast food, shopping centers, and subdivisions. Increasingly, even wilderness and the national parks are besieged to their very gates. Can this park, its neighbors ask, spur economic growth through greater tourism?

Under the railroads, there were practical limits in pursuing activities that cheapened the landscape, and preservation was not meant just for parks. In the East, where the city ended the country began—here lay the dairy farms and family gardens that directly fed the city. The countryside maintained an identity, without the shopping centers and subdivisions now robbing it of its distinctiveness. Most roads were two lanes instead of four, and most trips greater than 100 miles were still the purview of passenger trains.

The Lackawanna Railroad, with the shortest route between New York and Buffalo, hoped to attract additional passengers with the scenery; the company created the fictional character Phoebe Snow to enliven its advertising. Advertisement ca. 1905 (magazine unknown). Author's collection.

No wonder most older Americans recall with affection their first ride aboard a train. It was still the age of connectivity; movement still meant discovery. How could I forget my experience, since it involved a train called *Phoebe Snow*. Early in December 1952, Mother announced she had won a trip. Right after Christmas we would be taking the train and spending three days in New York. It was the only time in my life I could not wait for Christmas Day to end. Finally we were packed, and Father called a cab.

In those days, Binghamton, New York, called itself the Parlor City, priding itself on the beauty of its tree-lined boulevards. The largest employer, Endicott-Johnson Shoes, had donated lavishly to form spacious parks. I do not recall a street without sidewalks or not flanked by towering, overarching elms. Our ride to the station went down such streets. Although it was winter and the branches were bare, a hint of summer's warmth remained, and the porches and sidewalks overflowed with conversing neighbors. It is not that Binghamton had escaped city problems or that Norman Rockwell always got his paintings right. Binghamtonians knew the covers of the *Saturday Evening Post* were an ideal portrayal of American life, but still, there was a spirit to the city and its residents that came from the design of its neighborhoods.

We reached the station and began the principal experience of our trip. Then, railroads built stations inside a community, whereas now airports are built far distant from urban and residential centers. Binghamton had two stations, both in the heart of town. (Then, people still spoke of communities as having a "heart" or center.) Opposite the station of the Delaware, Lackawanna & Western Railroad stood the Arlington Hotel. It was another city favorite, assuring passengers exiting the station they need not wait to get a room. Downtown, with the best restaurants, shops, and theaters, was just a brief stroll away.

The station was surrounded by life. An arriving train, and especially the *Phoebe Snow,* was a ritual for everyone. The moment passersby heard her whistle, many joined us on the platform. Others took their places on the bridge that crossed the tracks, observing the hustle and excitement from above.

We might read far too much into the ritual, but what ritual has replaced it? In Binghamton, none—now that the trains are gone. Holiday parades are sporadic; the trains brought people together daily. In that bustle of comings and goings, the downtown was perpetually being nourished. Even business travel was considered a privilege, and those enjoying the world outside were somehow obligated to share the experience. Time spent today on a cell phone, a laptop computer, or watching airport CNN—time spent aloof from those around us—was then filled

The Lackawanna Railroad Station in Scranton, Pennsylvania, features thirty-six panels in the Beaux-Arts style. Panel 10 shows the Delaware Water Gap, after a painting by Clark G. Voorhees. (Photograph B-308, ca. 1910). Courtesy of Steamtown National Historic Site from the collection of Syracuse University.

with neighbors. Public space meant enjoying the opportunity to experience a world beyond home and self.

What I considered a once-in-a-lifetime opportunity—boarding the *Phoebe Snow* for New York—occurred daily at 2:00 PM. Now *we* stood among the passengers, the beneficiaries of my mother's luck. A local radio station had been running a promotion called Cinderella Weekend—the prize, round trip for four on the *Phoebe Snow* and two nights in Manhattan. Finalists faced off in the studio. Mother had won twice before but gave those trips away. I was bitterly disappointed, even when she explained—a dear friend with lung cancer needed hope, another getting married could not afford a honeymoon. Mother had insisted they deserved the trips more than we did, and simply vowed to win again.

THE ROUTE OF SCENIC BEAUTY

THE
Phoebe Snow
DAYLIGHT TRIP
New York - Buffalo

Lackawanna Railroad

Incredibly, she had, and here we were, climbing the steps of the *Phoebe Snow*! I was too young to know the history, or that the image of Phoebe awaiting passengers in the lounge car was created from an artist's imagination. Still, enough of her legend had come to life. In the decade before World War I, Phoebe had been the poster girl of the Lackawanna Railroad, her purpose to announce, in flirtatious jingles, that the railroad's locomotives burned anthracite coal. Unlike soft coal, anthracite burned much cleaner, sparing passengers at the rear from eating soot. Women especially had been reassured by Phoebe's original rhyme: "My gown stays white / From morn till night / Upon the Road of Anthracite."

The engines now were diesel, painted soft gray with a yellow nose. On a distant siding stood several locomotives waiting to be scrapped. No longer breathing steam, their somber hulks contrasted starkly with *Phoebe*'s livery. Maroon bands set off with yellow stripes swept rearward along the cars. The *Phoebe Snow* seemed to promise that the railroad's future would be even more memorable than its past.[3]

Certainly, our trip was beginning memorably. Even as Mother ushered my brother and me toward our seats, I was enchanted by some fragrance. Never again have I experienced it, as if to do so would rob me of a keepsake. Perhaps it was the smell of the steam heat mixing with the cushions, or the upholstery soaking up the sunlight—I still don't know. I recall only that when the *Phoebe Snow* started moving, the aroma was like a drug. Suddenly, even Binghamton began looking special, every landmark seen from the train in delightful reverse. The radio station had it right: this had to be Cinderella Weekend, and the *Phoebe Snow* was our coach to the palace ball.

My perspective broadened on the train, and I noticed something different about the men working up and down the aisles. Mother, in the words of the time, explained the men were Negro porters. Now these words have a negative connotation, suggesting a life of dead-end jobs. Years later, the porters themselves would set me straight. Then trains had been a place of opportunity for African Americans, and the means of settling their families in a better place.[4] After unionization and even before, the better jobs on the railroads had come with tips. Tips had

---

In 1949, the name Phoebe Snow and the scenery of the Lackawanna Railroad were linked by naming a train after her. Referencing travel times and mileposts, the inside of this 1951 leaflet alerted passengers to the sights. Author's collection.

closed the disparity between their wages and the income generally enjoyed by whites. With the passenger train virtually gone, many of these workers had picked up slivers of their former jobs in airports and hotels. The majority I met were shining shoes. Regardless, they considered their careers with the railroads a privilege, allowing them to escape the poverty and racism of the South.

Although in 1952 that history escaped me, I sensed that the *Phoebe Snow* was in good hands. Men in black pants and white jackets lifted suitcases, waited tables, and answered a string of questions. A former porter in Seattle said, "We heard nothing about drugs and drive-by shootings in those days, did we?" That testimonial really got me thinking. He believed the railroads had given him direction. Both his rivals and his community had looked up to him. It mattered not in the least that his prosperity was due to tips; railroad jobs were coveted. He had bought a house, raised three children, and put all of them through college. Then the railroads fell apart, and with them the prestige he had enjoyed. The airlines were looking for single, attractive women—young women—not grown men needing good wages to build strong families.

We also forget the communities that paid the price of the loss of the railroads. Wherever trains had been stocked or serviced, whole neighborhoods had grown around them. Now those neighborhoods languished, a prelude to slums and crime. Although Binghamton was not a principal railroad endpoint, it did load passengers, freight, and mail. Sleeping-car passengers enjoyed what were known as "setouts." Here the sleeping car, waiting on a siding, might be boarded ahead of an arriving train, or conversely, could be dropped there in the middle of the night, allowing passengers to sleep until a decent hour.[5] All these jobs, principally performed by African Americans, provided a middle-class lifestyle. Dare we suggest that the civil rights movement (like the environmentalists), missed an opportunity in the 1960s by not calling forcefully for the preservation of America's passenger trains?

In the same manner, landscapes opened by the railroads and extolled as scenic lost the steward that had wished them whole. After all, a scenic

The back cover of the leaflet *The Route of Scenic Beauty* invites the *Phoebe Snow*'s passengers to partake in "intelligent observation" and, in this 1951 printing, to be mindful of the railroad's centennial. Note the durability of the Phoebe jingle, now fifty years old: "Each mile is quite a new delight...." Author's collection.

LACKAWANNA RAILROAD

1851 = One Hundred Years = 1951

The pleasure of any trip is always enhanced by intelligent observation. A few words of explanation to the uninformed traveler frequently lend an added charm and interest to an already attractive scene.

The route of the Lackawanna Railroad is rich in *scenic* and *historic* interest, and this folder has been prepared for the purpose of familiarizing the traveler with such information as may serve to heighten the charm of a trip over the line. Its aim is to add to your pleasure and perhaps prove instructive.

In the limitations of a folder of this size, it is impossible to do more than touch upon the more interesting and important physical features of the railroad and the country through which it passes.

The Lackawanna Railroad is the shortest line between New York City and Buffalo, forming a double-track steel boulevard 396 miles in length between these two cities. In this distance, it passes through the states of New Jersey, Pennsylvania and New York, crossing six important rivers and three mountain chains in its course.

It's time to go with Phoebe Snow
And view the scenes she loves to show
Each mile is quite a new delight
Upon the Road of Anthracite

THE ROUTE OF

A deck of *Phoebe Snow* playing cards from the 1950s reminds passengers to watch for the Tunkhannock Viaduct. Author's collection.

EXTRA

JOKER

TUNKHANNOCK VIADUCT
THE WORLD'S LARGEST CONCRETE BRIDGE

The Tunkhannock Viaduct, on the Lackawanna Railroad's main line between New York and Buffalo, is situated 22 miles west of Scranton and 40 miles east of Binghamton.

The structure crosses the valley of Tunkhannock Creek, near the town of Nicholson, Pa. It is the largest concrete railroad bridge in the world — 2,375 feet in length, 240 feet above the Valley, and 300 feet above bed rock foundations.

JOKER

EXTRA

route could be sold for its scenic value, as elegantly recalled in the palatial waiting room of the Scranton station. When the building opened in 1908, the railroad's publicist was quick to announce, "Probably its most striking decorative feature is the thirty-six faience panels in colors after the painting of Clark G. Voorhees, the well-known landscape artist. These panels were reproduced in color direct from Nature and represent actual scenes along the line of the Lackawanna Railroad."[6]

Although the station is now a hotel—with the former waiting room its central lobby—the panels have been preserved. The hotel pleasantly reminds guests what the panels are. Less obvious is their original purpose: promoting landscape as an asset. Not told is what happened to America's landscapes once the railroads began to fold. Under the railroad's aegis, engineering was all about aesthetics—hugging rivers, following valleys, and searching the mountains for an easy grade. The railroads took full advantage, inviting passengers to immerse in all of it. Aboard the trains, timetables, guidebooks, playing cards, and menu covers extolled scenery and natural history. Posters, calendars, and magazine ads invited revisiting the theme at home, and best of all, the railroads flooded America's mailboxes with most of it for free.

In contrast, advertising today rarely mentions scenery, let alone promotes the welfare of featured landscapes. The subservience of the land is understood. What the railroads sold for enjoyment is now for consumption only. The land is just a backdrop, inviting the consumer to focus on the object being peddled, whether it is soap, beer, or cars.

Whatever their motive (and it was business, surely), the railroads resisted advertising that seemed exploitative. We may grant it was a different age, in which even the wealthy were traveling by rail. Tasteless advertising was not a draw. Nonetheless, in their appeal to the high end of public opinion, the railroads invited the rest of the public to follow suit. Whether the railroads followed opinion or made it, the benefits for conservation were still the same. Initially criticized for building destructively (the "machine in the garden" imagery), the railroads had imaginatively turned the tables. They disagreed with critics like Henry David Thoreau, asserting that natural beauty could be preserved while building railroads. In that case, preserving the natural environment made absolute sense. The more landmarks a railroad featured in daylight hours, the better its chances for beating the competition.

In major cities, too, the construction of terminals called for grandeur—a station shouldn't be merely elegant, it should be monumental. Most railroads felt obligated to copy Rome. The admitted exceptions to beauty, where trains passed through industrial areas, might also have their appeal. At the very least, factories and smokestacks were weirdly fascinating, especially when viewed at night. Their magic was in their use-fulness. Much as farms and villages were sold as ennobling, the industrial landscape displayed progress on the march.

It was my good fortune that in 1952 much of that age still survived. Mass consumerism remained in the future; at least the Lackawanna Railroad had not succumbed. Everything about the *Phoebe Snow* still invited passengers to think of landscape as the American dream. Where the man-made environment complemented the landscape, the results were striking too. The Lackawanna promised we would cross the great Tunkhannock Viaduct. Table mats and brochures told its story, noting that early in the century the railroad had needed to straighten and modernize its right-of-way. A valley northwest of Scranton, Pennsylvania, cut defiantly across the route. The railroad planned a monumental bridge to span it, fashioned from concrete and structural steel. Even as the viaduct rose, it, like the *Phoebe Snow,* towered to legendary status in its own right, ten graceful arches linked for half a mile between opposing bulwarks of ancient bedrock.

Mother read the brochures, then asked the porter for a clue—how could we tell when we were close? "There is a first bridge, only shorter," he replied, "we get to the big one soon after that." Was there still enough time to make it to the dining car and enjoy a late lunch with our view? "Yes, ma'am," he said again, smiling broadly at our eagerness. "You still have twenty minutes." Pleased, Mother took my brother and me by the hand and led us back to find a table.

As advertised, the Tunkhannock Viaduct took our breath away—our noses were pressed against the window. A winter sun flooded the valley 250 feet below. Groves of trees spilled shadows against the abutments, as if threatening to shake us down. It was less than a minute of my life—probably no longer than thirty seconds—but no seat in a dining car (and no tuna sandwich) has been more memorable to this day.

After lunch, we made our way to the lounge car, where my father had claimed a booth. Now at the rear of the train, we observed the engines sweeping gracefully into every turn. We snaked into the Lackawanna Valley, boarding passengers in downtown Scranton, then in a mottle of gathering clouds resumed our place among the ridge tops. Flecks of snow and deepening shadows marked our passage through the leafless, whitened Poconos, the train still arcing left and right, on pace for the Delaware Water Gap, the New Jersey cutoff, and the connecting ferry for New York.

Such images remain in the popular memory, not just in mine, recalling what the passenger train offered landscape. As the country ages, those memories die, but not the truth of what trains do. The country would like to think it has built past the railroad, but it has not built past the need. Respect for the natural world can hardly flourish if the technological world incites its absence.

So I am reminded by my trip on the *Phoebe Snow* that the railroads, transporting many people and employing others, elevated the world for everyone. Railroads made the landscape part of the journey; indeed, they helped keep the landscape whole. The *Phoebe Snow* herself pledged "the route of scenic beauty" and "the route of scenic charm." That was neither ecology nor environmentalism speaking, but certainly it was a start. Could there be any better reason for restoring the passenger train? Think again about what took its place.

What Europe Is Teaching Still

Consider that Europe is never grounded, either by weather or by terrorists. Nor would it be grounded by a shortage of oil. Most of its railroads have been fully electrified; hydroelectric power abounds in the Alps and Pyrenees. The same might be said of Japan, as both are far advanced when it comes to trains. But Europe remains our model because America looks there for the cultural lessons of a shared, historical past.

Still, few Americans will willingly admit the lesson until they have ridden Europe's trains. Then, even Americans would agree: Europe's railroads are magnificent. I didn't realize how magnificent until June 1982, when I bought a rail pass and flew to Frankfurt. I planned to visit my brother, a captain in the U.S. Army, but otherwise intended to ride a broad sample of Europe's trains. I was astounded just by their frequency. I had always believed (doesn't every American?) that the United States has the best of everything. Then I found myself zipping from Germany into Switzerland on a train Americans would have thought luxurious—for Europe it was only average. And I could have taken one of fifty other trains that very same day. I finally grasped the geography holding America hostage—the wilderness of ocean on either side of us. It is perhaps not our stubbornness or complacency after all. Before we can make the proper choices, we need to realize what they are.

Even in the aftermath of September 11, Americans have slipped comfortably back into the notion that isolation is all we need, seeing isolation (in the military sense rather than cultural) as a national security issue. Rail pass in hand, I saw the technological side of isolation, how it robs us as a culture of a daily incentive to weigh our choices against the world's. In Europe, countries have learned to cooperate. Proximity alone provides a wealth of opportunities to see how one's neighbors think and operate. Switzerland took my breath away, and not just because its railroads glorify the Alps. Outside my window, roses climbed the gates of factories, flower boxes spilled over the windows of every house. Germany and Austria were also filled with gardens, often flush with the tracks on either side. English, virtually Europe's second language, was spoken throughout the trains, and it was not uncommon for conductors and students to know three or four languages with equal fluency.

It is no wonder that European cohesiveness includes transportation, and railroads are no exception. Think of it: thousands of passenger trains crisscross the borders of Europe every day. The United States has two extensive borders, one with Canada, the other Mexico. But where, along either border, is there a level of cooperation even remotely resembling Europe's? The trains America might otherwise have come to emulate are still thousands of miles away.

If that distance is no deterrent to the airplane, to the pocketbook it remains a gulf. Even as tourists, Americans spend barely enough time in Europe to experience what trains do around the clock. Nor are television and the Internet any substitute for actually visiting those trains in person. When on business, Americans rarely stay in Europe long enough to learn the culture. Even those traveling for pleasure tend to dismiss the incredible efficiency of Europe's railroads as a "foreign thing." Simply, American culture encourages us to see most foreign technology as inferior.

Physical isolation cements the perception that America is more advanced. How could the United States be behind in anything? Returning home, I tried explaining a city like Frankfurt that has fifteen hundred passenger trains *every day*. Most of my friends dismissed me, simply declaring that cars were better. No doubt I was the one mistaken. It was just that Europe, unable to "afford" cars, was "forced" to have more trains, and that Europe was out of room (as if room only means territory). Other friends wrongly argued that Europe had no superhighways. Never having been to Europe, none of my friends felt intimidated by the facts. Their assumption was not that Europeans had wisely preserved a range of choices, but rather that Americans had picked the best choice.

When we as Americans, disdaining a true comparative, argue that Europe is more compact, we are merely finalizing our preferred excuse for

Across Europe, railroads display a sensitivity to human scale and landscape rarely seen in the United States. Playground and narrow gauge railroad in Gstaad, Switzerland, October 1999. Photograph by the author.

not having passenger trains that serve the continent. Europe's trains serve a densely populated, small-scale geography. Europe needs trains, we argue; we don't. Americans flatly deny the possibility that Europeans simply prefer good trains.

Density matters, to be sure. But how does it explain so many trains? Daily, every citizen and every tourist has hundreds of trains from which to choose. Even the smallest towns have several trains a day. The explanation lies in history, not merely geography or population. Europe knows civilization to be a veneer, requiring stewardship with every moment. In the twentieth century, two world wars and the Cold War—with Europe then split by the Iron Curtain—brutally reminded Europe that maintaining civilization is a full-time job.

The point is that Europe sees transportation differently—as a way to encourage human interaction. It is when Europeans have stopped communicating with one another that tragedy has struck. Now the United States, too, has the tragedy of the World Trade Center reduced to ruins. What Europe questions is not America's enthusiasm, innate goodness, or generosity. Europe remembers who invaded Normandy and who paid for the Marshall Plan. What Europe questions is America's tendency to think of civilization as immediacy. How is it that Americans, thinking in the present moment, believe that tomorrow will come on their terms?

The point remains that Europe, recalling its history, is less optimistic. What matters is cultural cement. Railroads are cultural cement—they help people learn to be friends instead of enemies. It is a subtlety, perhaps, that only a European could know. Then again, consider the new divisions in America: the "blue" states versus the "red" states. As America's elections get sharper and ever nastier, what is happening to our cement?

What Americans have come to see as conformity—the railroads—Europeans see as unity. In a typical city, subway lines and streetcars connect with a centralized railroad station; dozens more connect with the airport. All act like a giant web. By design, the system operates in every direction, connecting a city's peripheries to its core.

Significantly, there is still a core, something demanding a cultural focus. Suburbs may spill one into the other, and still their transportation will form a core. Stations remain centralized, maintaining the broadest possible ties with the urban landscape.

To be sure, the car plays an important role, and Europeans accept that its role will grow. But just because the automobile is the latest technology is no excuse for dropping railroads. Especially for the maintenance and preservation of central cities, the efficiency of rail-based transportation is too good to throw away.

Of course, my friends were partially right. World War II limited Europe's choices. Its soldiers, returning to broken countries, found devastation everywhere. Cities and factories were bombed-out hulks. In the United States, GI's returned to an industrial giant, marvelously untouched. American companies could not wait to convert back to peacetime goods. After four years with nothing to buy, America had pent-up savings in banks and war bonds. The first thing Rosie the Riveter and her GI husband wanted was a car. Next came the house in the suburbs, assisted by government loans. As a result, pressure mounted to build more highways, leading to the splurge of road-building that ended with the Interstate Highway System.

After the war, Europe rebuilt collectively, continuing its mastery of public transportation through the 1950s and 1960s. Meanwhile, America contentedly forgot even the fundamentals, with most larger cities abandoning streetcars and trolleys as fast as the passenger train, ensuring that Americans would no long think of rail. Led by a triumvirate of competitive interests—automobiles, oil, and rubber—the vast majority of urban rail lines were surreptitiously purchased and cities convinced to rip them out.[1]

With the decline of that connectivity in the United States, Europe would say a piece of America's unity died as well. Finally, whether downtown or in the suburbs, the passenger train had no base. Suffering from the lack of local and regional coordination, intercity trains inevitably declined for lack of patrons. Typically, city bus lines had their own stations; connectivity with the railroads did not exist.

By the 1970s, what Amtrak touted as proof of a renaissance proved more rhetorical than revolutionary. But it was not just Amtrak's fault. Everyone—citizens, business leaders, and politicians—had forgotten the meaning of connectivity. Taking the train was only part of it; getting to and from the station was an equal part. By now, Americans could not even imagine Europe's diversity of connecting services, truly a public utility of vast proportions.

Nor do Americans, still thinking as individuals, fully grasp why that system appears so seamless. Foremost, the public is expected to contribute by looking out for itself. No official stands in the doorway quizzing every passenger about the rules. Safety is everyone's responsibility; "Watch Your Step" means exactly that. Although Europe protects the rights of individuals, it remains a shared responsibility. In no-nonsense fashion, the government has agreed to operate the trains, but only so long as the passengers do their part.

Thus, even as Europe's highways and cars have multiplied, it has aggressively modernized its railroads too. As history shows us, Europe believes in protecting all its options. Only America equates the right to travel with conspicuous consumption; Europe insists that the traveler be a citizen. The need to get from place to place is respected, but the traveler is asked to respect a sense of place.

For Americans, the constant pitting of economics against responsibility means our system is hard to change. Other values go unrecognized because they cannot possibly pay their way (or so we argue). In that vein, the distinguished ecologist Aldo Leopold summed up the problem using the environment as his example. The "basic weakness in a conservation system based wholly on economic motives is that most members of the land community have no economic value," he noted. "Wildflowers and songbirds are examples." In Leopold's native Wisconsin, he estimated that less than 5 percent of its plants and animals "can be sold, fed, eaten, or otherwise put to economic use. Yet these creatures are members of the

Europe believes in protecting all its options: the government runs the trains, but the passengers must do their part. Intercity European express train ready for boarding, Frankfurt, Germany, September 1999. Photograph by the author.

biotic community, and if (as I believe) its stability depends on its integrity, they are entitled to continuance."[2]

In America railroads, like Leopold's wildflowers and songbirds, have failed some commercial test. A final resorting to fiscal subterfuge demands that every label support those findings. Railroads get taxpayer "subsidies" while new highways are built with "trust funds." The point of such pejorative labeling is to head off the system we no longer want. Because the economy now "trusts" in highways, their costs (and taxation) may be excused. If the tax is one we have approved, we find a way not to call it a tax. We rationalize a superior legitimacy—only something old would need a subsidy. Life is better now, the labeling settles in, all invention since the outdated railroad is more progressive—indeed, innately so.

"Are you from the United States?" the companion in my compartment asked. By now, I welcomed someone breaking into my thoughts, reminding me to enjoy myself. I immediately noticed her disappointment as I tried answering her in German. "Your German is very good [she was kind], but may I practice on you my English?" A college student, she had recently visited the United States, spending a week in Glacier National Park. She confessed that what had impressed her was the space. "Montana is so big! And less than a million people, no? All that is gone from Germany years ago."

I had to ask, "And did you miss anything while in the United States?" Of course, she had missed the trains. "Travel in America is so difficult without a car. Europe would never allow that, if only to attract more tourists."

I confessed tourism to be my purpose, and agreed—if I were driving, what would I see? Alone, I would be watching the road. "But in Germany, you would not be alone, racing us on the autobahn!" she laughed. "Which you do," I replied, "and for which any American would get a ticket, but despite all of it you have your railroads. What is the explanation for that?" "Why would we not have them?" she answered, now visibly perplexed that I did not seem to understand. "They are good for us, how did I say before? Tourists come here because we have trains. Besides, not every German drives."

There it was: "Why would we not have them?" America has allowed itself to argue just the opposite—that railroads, as an existing technology, invariably have less value. Europe believes in a value-added society, in which every new technology proves its worth by complementing what exists. Europeans know that picking winners and losers does more than displace the loser—it further destroys the cultural fabric of what had been painstakingly built before. As clearly as anyone, Europe saw that the horse and buggy were worthy of displacement. There are no more ox carts or Roman chariots anywhere on Europe's roads. But why displace the railroad? It has not even entered Europe's mind.

I settled back in my seat, finally putting my thoughts to rest. Europe was not a better place, just a wiser place, because it knows the reasons for having trains.

Dismemberment and Farewell

With few exceptions, rail passenger service in the United States fell apart in the 1960s. In Binghamton, the decade dawned with the merger of the Erie and Lackawanna railroads. Afterward known as the Erie–Lackawanna, the new company promised shippers and passengers a better future, eliminating the redundancy of two railroads where one might now suffice. But was it true? Suddenly, the *Phoebe Snow* lost her name, and her popular lounge cars were dropped. Both backfired with the public, and in 1963 her name and lounges were restored. However, *Phoebe* no longer stopped at Buffalo, having been routed on the former Erie line to Chicago. At least Buffalo, via the New York Central, still had full connections east and west. If Binghamton lost service on the Erie–Lackawanna, both the city and the counties across southern New York would have no other train. Then the incredible happened: on a crisp, clear autumn day in November 1966, Miss Phoebe—aged seventeen years—said farewell to the Southern Tier.[1]

One full-service train still survived—the *Lake Cities,* a vestige of the Erie Railroad. However, if the *Phoebe Snow* could be dropped, the *Lake Cities* hardly seemed safe. After all, its eastbound schedule reeked of inconvenience, arriving in Binghamton at 4:00 in the morning rather than 2:00 in the afternoon. Westbound it arrived close to midnight, compared to

Phoebe's appearance at 3:00 PM. Talk already floated of a conspiracy. The best-scheduled and most popular train was gone, leaving a stepsister to fill her place. Although equipped with a diner/lounge and sleeper, the *Lake Cities* was hardly the *Phoebe Snow*. For Binghamton (and Elmira, whose stop preceded it), the *Lake Cities* defied common sense, requiring that anyone bound for New York roll out of bed between 2:00 and 3:00 AM.

Even then, it was pointless calling the station to ask if the train would be on time. Either there was a constant busy signal, or no one picked up the phone. Like the scheduling, the tactic was ominous, intended to discourage last-minute passengers; how could it be otherwise? Passengers either arrived in time for the scheduled departure or risked missing the only train that day. No one dared bet on the probability that the train would be hours late. Although the train westbound from New York was more convenient, phoning the station was still a gamble. At least that train was just five hours old and might arrive on time. The eastbound *Lake Cities* departed from Chicago, with nearly 800 miles to throw broken signals, freight trains, or other problems into its way.

I kept hearing the warnings from my friend Walter Smith, an engineer with the railroad. The *Lake Cities,* like the *Phoebe Snow,* was being set up for a petition to the Interstate Commerce Commission (ICC). Dear Commissioners: Do you expect the Erie-Lackawanna to operate a passenger train that no one wants to ride? "We had better ride," Walt admonished, "while we have the chance." With or without Walt at my side, I was a frequent passenger until January 1970, when his prediction was confirmed. My farewell trip was Christmas 1969, traveling eastbound from Bloomington, Illinois. A new graduate student at Illinois State University, I braved a postmidnight departure on the Gulf, Mobile & Ohio Railroad, arriving in Chicago at Union Station just past 5:00 AM.

My transfer to Dearborn Station was the easy part. There followed an seemingly interminable wait before the *Lake Cities* pulled out at 11:00 AM. With the few other diehards, I practiced the familiar ritual—slouching myself across the benches, faking sleep, and drinking endless cups of coffee. I read and reread a stack of papers. The pain was still worth it, I thought. After all, that petition to the ICC was in, and perhaps had already been approved. Next year Binghamton would be stranded. Likely, I would not be going home by train again for a good many years to come.

When we finally departed from Chicago, the *Lake Cities* pulled just two coaches and a baggage car. The diner and sleeper would be added later. I daydreamed over the receding skyline and felt the train slowly gaining speed. Soon we were in Indiana going 70 mph, and I had forgotten how tired I really was. Our passage now pleasantly alternated between open forests and ranks of farms. What beautiful, productive country, I thought. And what a beautiful young woman (I had suddenly noticed!) seated immediately across the aisle.

Too late, I said to myself, she probably thinks I am just a rail nut. I wished I had not done so much rubbernecking, hearing the rumble of passing freights. At least I had a perfect excuse to turn in her direction, and when I turned again caught her smiling. Did she know it had been a feint? No matter, she asked the perfect question—my purpose on the train. "Heading home for Christmas," I said. "And you?" "The same," she replied, then added, "and where is home for you?" "Binghamton, New York," I answered. Her next answer would tell me if this was too good to be true. And where was she was getting off? (Please God, not Indiana!) "Hoboken," she said, and I could not believe my luck. "Yes," she confirmed, "last stop." A student at Wheaton College in Illinois, Ellen planned on spending the holidays with her family in New Jersey.

So it was possible we could be together my entire trip. Now, how had Cary Grant played the part? I was not Cary Grant, and this was not the *Twentieth Century Limited,* and we were not in a movie, after all. But this train would be getting a dining car at Huntington, Indiana. The rest was up to me. "Did you know they are about to add the dining car?" I asked. "We can watch it from the rear. Better yet, would you care to join me during lunch?" Ellen's smile and thank you, she would love to, reassured me Cary Grant could not have done it better.

The wonderful thing about half-full trains is never feeling rushed. In the dining car we sat until 4:00 PM, only then returning to our seats. There we talked away the rest of the afternoon. Like all young people in the 1960s, we hardly lacked topics, from our majors in college to the civil rights movement to the war in Vietnam. Finally, sensing the deepening twilight, I realized the dining car would be serving dinner. Would she again join me? I asked, now confident her answer would be yes. The waiter seated us, adjusted the flowers, and promised to hurry back. Outside, the farmhouses blinking to life as darkness descended added the perfect romantic touch.

Returning, our waiter suggested the turkey special. "No need to hurry," he reassured us, then flashed a knowing smile. "The dinner is four courses, and you can take all the time you like." Such was the gift of a Christmas railroad trip, to linger over dessert and coffee. Afterwards, I took forever to pay the bill. There would come another distraction, another enchanted town, its gables and steeples ablaze with lights. Then the wisps of snow were suddenly back, their dance crazed by the rushing train. Other flakes climbed the window, catching the glow of the lights behind them. We sat spellbound, unwilling to move, as if our slightest twitching would end the magic.

Finally, it did end, the diner closed, and even our waiter's smile had faded. With my receipt and change came his chilling reminder that the *Lake Cities* would soon be gone. Ellen would fly back to Illinois, and I would drive if the train's end came before my vacation's. We had many wonderful hours still ahead, talking and dozing in our coach. But somehow the darkness had lost its romance and the lights no longer soothed. Then it was time for me to leave. At Binghamton, Ellen walked me to the vestibule and hugged me before I stepped into the snow. Outside the train for the first time in hours, I noticed it was covered with ice, in places dropping icicles beneath the windows as if the coaches were shedding tears. I managed to look back only once. So that was it, I thought to myself, the last Christmas on the route of the *Phoebe Snow*. There would be no more dining cars offering romance, dusted in the sparkle of Christmas snowflakes.

Indeed, the *Lake Cities* barely survived past New Year's. I had decided to drive back to Illinois regardless, since the date had not been exact. My mother sent me the clipping from our local newspaper, listing the usual claims. Of course, the railroad held others responsible. There was too little mail and too few passengers, too many new highways and modern airports. All I felt was a sinking emptiness that something so wonderful was gone for good.

At least Ellen and I had the memory, comforted that our experience had ended nobly. True, the upholstery on our seats was looking threadbare, and the frame of our coach seemed completely shot. And passengers still could not get through to the station to ask if the train would be on time. Nonetheless, our dining car had been set to perfection, and each of our meals had been served as a main event. Although the railroad wanted no more to do with passengers, it had treated us holdouts well.

Retracing those miles by highway, I invariably reflected on the differences between cars and trains. The same romantic diversions aboard a train could be a deadly act on the highway. I did all my reflecting facing front, but while crossing a bridge in Indiana I felt the car spin perilously on a patch of ice. Of course, the sign said Bridge Freezes Before Road Surface. There had been none of those worries aboard the train. Finally,

It is 1968 and the dinner menu of the *Lake Cities* still features the Tunkhannock Viaduct. Although the Erie-Lackawanna petitioned to annul the train in 1969, the railroad's heritage has a surviving influence. Author's collection.

ERIE LACKAWANNA RAILWAY COMPANY

DINING SERVICE

Dinner Menu

"Erie Lackawanna spectacular 50 year old Tunkhannock Viaduct at Nicholson,
Penna. — One of the railroad engineering wonders of the world."

The Friendly Service Route

having missed the last string of guardrails, I calmed myself and went deep in thought. What would the absence of trains mean for cities? Even as the monotony of the highway repossessed me, my thinking stayed the same. I thought of downtown Binghamton, already changed. Businesses historically centered around the station had retreated to the suburbs. It reminded me of the Chinese proverb of death by a thousand cuts. It seemed that as each passenger train died, another piece of Binghamton died as well. Automakers claimed that the car had freed the city; I saw only the dismemberment of all I knew.

The suburbs had many supporters, each arguing the irrelevance of aging city cores. Suburbanites were willing exiles and frankly preferred their cars. Perhaps. But what did it mean to allow an entire industry to simply vanish? What if, years or decades down the road, the road itself became obsolete? As it stood, the first oil shock was only three years away, and no one in 1970 was predicting that. Meanwhile, Europe had not allowed its central cities to collapse but instead was strengthening them with trains. Only Americans seemed to feel rich enough—and confident enough—to tear apart railroads and rebuild for cars.

Predictably, Binghamton had joined the great majority. Now, if only Binghamton could "capture" a shopping mall or two. That would make up for losing sixteen thousand jobs in manufacturing and all those railroad jobs. The city needed only to make room for shopping malls, just as the suburbs were doing. And so the mayor called out the wrecking ball; all those "obsolete" buildings would have to make way for parking lots.

In hindsight, that was the period that spawned historic preservation; in New York City, it was highlighted by the criminal loss of Penn Station. For me, the rubble of Binghamton's Arlington Hotel, like Penn Station, confirmed what happens when trains are lost. The first thing that goes is the synergy. Tearing out the Arlington was not the problem; losing the trains that had served it was the problem. The one without the other was meaningless—both were the reason people had loved downtown. Now, without the *Phoebe Snow* (and later the *Lake Cities*) to bring them *into* town, the Arlington Hotel was stranded.

If Binghamton could not fill the Arlington's space, what then? Sure enough, the businesses surrounding it began folding as well. Occasionally, some developer ventured a grand pronouncement, then as quickly reneged and walked away. Too late, people realized that demolishing buildings accomplished nothing. No one had ventured a trip to Europe or had learned from their experience. What Binghamton needed—what the nation needed—was not to throw away its past.

Granted, that past was not viable everywhere, and cities, in their essence, are places of constant change. But cities are also where people gather and so must consider what they gather for. I imagined the writings of Frederick Law Olmsted and William Whyte languishing somewhere in the Binghamton Public Library.[2] What makes a city a desirable gathering place and preserves its beauty too? Europe knows the key is public transportation; only a few American cities know that. Binghamton needed visionaries, not just promoters. It takes more than demolition—and starting over—to preserve a city's heart.

It remains America's willingness to throw off the old for the new that still surprises Europeans. Although Binghamton was changing and fast losing its industries to the South, the city had obviously existed for other reasons. Exploring such reasons had been Europe's answer to the question of why not eliminate the railroads. A city can reinvent itself as long as its infrastructure remains intact. In the United States, San Francisco is the best example of a city (with a European flair) that reinvented itself around a usable past. Because it kept its cable cars and restored urban trolleys, residents and tourists still delight in the traditional neighborhoods that made the city famous.

Elsewhere, the developers invading city hall had methodically preached the opposite, insisting that cities condemn any neighborhood or park happening to stand in the way of progress. That period of defiance—of disdain for beauty and public transportation—is like no other in American history. At one point in the 1960s, developers and highway engineers had designs on every urban park in the country: open space was wasted space. Even the most powerful railroads had not believed urban beauty was expendable.

Rather railroads, conceding their limitations, had forced development to concede them too. Entering Binghamton, the Lackawanna and Erie railroads followed the Susquehanna River in search of easy grades. Developers were given a choice—either languish or follow the tracks. Then came the highways, countering those limitations, and all aesthetic bets were off. Grades finally meant nothing to developers, who pushed the city into the hills. There went Mother's berry patch and Father's secret overlook; there went my favorite brook. The views from the houses taking their place were stunning, but the essential point remained: whole hillsides had been disfigured. Binghamton's railroads had insisted the city be a preservationist, if only by default.

In contrast, European railroads, building past their earlier limitations, had still been expected to conform. Consequently, even standard-gauge mountain railroads possessed the qualities of narrow roads. To be sure, Europe did not forbid development; rather, engineers invented railroads appropriate to each new setting. In Switzerland, for example, hillside farming motivated the use of cog-assisted railroads. Following the contours of fields and pastures, each allowed cattle to graze right up to the tracks. Cuts and fills were avoided. Otherwise, Europe itself kept building highways. Europeans tried minimalist construction first and did so far more consistently.

Because few things about suburban development in the United States are minimalist, aging cities have aged further still. Inexorably, the retreat to the suburbs lent legitimacy to the railroads' argument that America had forever soured on the passenger train. Even where initially served by railroads, bedroom communities now depended on the car. Few politicians insisted that new development include historic ties with existing railroads.

One of the notable exceptions was Claiborne Pell, whose book *Megalopolis Unbound* was published in 1966. Because Pell was a United States senator, it seemed the book would be widely read. Whether it would be widely heeded remained the point. The book's focus was the Northeast Corridor, where the Penn-Central Railroad (the latest merger of the Pennsylvania and the New York Central) shortly afterward agreed to a new generation of high-speed trains.[3] But what about the rest of the country? In 1967 a new organization, the National Association of Railroad Passengers (NARP), underscored that need and campaigned (as its name suggested) for a *national* rail passenger system. However, another book by the journalist Peter Lyon warned NARP of an uphill battle. America had gone "to hell in a day coach," Lyon reasoned, and the railroads had speeded up the process.[4]

Simply put, once the railroad companies had determined that freight was more profitable, passengers had to go. And, after a century of dominating American transportation, railroads resented anyone even questioning that assertion. But their plan backfired on them and the nation. Now that Americans actually had a choice of transportation, they did just as the railroads asked and switched to cars and planes. But in the rush to highways and airports, Americans decided the railroads were outdated in all respects. After all, freight could move on highways too. Politically, the railroads needed a positive image; instead, most adopted the role of victim. Eventually, the more the railroads claimed this role the more they believed it. In this final, debilitating argument, all thought of cooperation was tossed aside.

A final retrenchment seemed in order. Their future, as the railroads came to see it, was in transporting goods that others refused to transport: coal, grain, and chemicals topped the list. Railroads looked to be indispensable for everything that could not be trucked or flown. Anything time-sensitive (and therefore troublesome), the railroads ultimately did not wish to keep.

Even in freight, the railroads seemed willing to sacrifice their historical connection with the public—the first-class mail and fast express.
Again, our family's experience was not unusual. On June 27, 1958, my
father's body came home from New York City in the express car of the
Phoebe Snow. Two days earlier, while visiting friends, he had died of a heart
attack in Bridgeport, Connecticut. Mother and I went to the station to
watch as the funeral home offloaded the casket into the hearse. This time,
we were at the front of the train, beside a car marked Railway Express
Agency. Next in line came the Railway Post Office. Both depended on
Phoebe's speed. In the 1960s, rather than fight to keep those markets—the
head-end business, as it was called—most railroads, having determined to
shed their passengers, became resigned to losing it all.

From one negative assumption—passengers are burdensome—many
others had begun to spring. What was the passenger train, if not another
freight train in which passengers brought up the rear? Except for the true
luxury trains in America, that was nearly always the case. Granted, the Post
Office Department would move to zip codes, and mail handling would
change forever. But the need to move the mail would never change, nor
would the need to transport bodies and other perishables that needed only
reasonable service and reasonable speed. But the railroads seemed willing
to give up all that just to prove the passenger train was losing money.

National policy (enamored of the competition) was then to accept
the mess the railroads were making of themselves. Certainly, few in the
industry saw any reason to step forward and save their passengers. A rare
exception, Robert Young of the Baltimore & Ohio, initially called for restoration of passenger service but is better remembered for later reneging.[5]
Railroad presidents usually addressed the problem by insisting that the
government, by fueling competitors, had become the enemy of all trains.

Obviously, if the railroads could build that case, the events sweeping
down on them were not inevitable. National leadership might have intervened had the railroads honestly asked for help. Instead, the railroads
kept disparaging the public. A century of arrogance had built a culture
where management resented change—and government. The railroads had
their formula, and would try it no matter what.

Railroads predicted that their costs would fall if they became freight
railroads only. It would no longer be necessary, for example, to bank
tracks on sharper curves—the outside rail elevated and the inside lowered
to reduce centrifugal force. Slower-moving freight trains hardly required
that concern. Coal and grain would survive at any speed, and even survive
derailments. Only with passenger trains did the railroads need to worry
about jolting coffee into someone's lap, or worse, face passengers suing
for lack of maintenance.

Avoiding duplication through mergers became another major strategy. Historically, railroads in the Northeast and Midwest had been overbuilt. Finally, the decline of those regions' industries encouraged the railroads to reduce capacity. Their principal argument was legitimate: why pay the extra taxes? Similarly, where railroads ran parallel and served identical markets, choosing one right-of-way made sense. West of Binghamton, for example, the Erie and Lackawanna railroads paralleled each other for miles, the Erie on the north bank of the Susquehanna River and the Lackawanna on the south. The lines averaged barely half a mile apart. It was a redundancy no longer necessary, so the merging lines tore up the Lackawanna tracks.

Unfortunately, the railroads across the nation then added a debilitating argument: why stop there? Generally, the portion surviving remained double track. But gradually, even that was considered a redundancy, and management called for a single line. Afterwards, even if the railroads had agreed to restore frequent, high-end service, the die was cast against it. Like Peter Lyon, I could not imagine a railroad acting against the future, or the government failing to intervene.

It is sobering, even today, to think of those prejudices in light of history. What other culture, what other government, gave in so methodically to the demise of railroads? Beyond the visual evidence—the stacked rails and ties—it was a transition I had come to know by ear. As a child, I had heard the trains speeding out of Binghamton, rattling the windows of our house a mile away. By the time I left college, ten years after the Erie-Lackawanna merger, Binghamton had grown strangely quiet. The absence of sound—of steel meeting steel—not only announced the passage of fewer trains, but also meant that the railroad, finally cutting into maintenance, had no choice but reduce the speeds.

Why talk about railroads as saviors of the American countryside when the tracks were all torn up? Why talk about high-speed trains for America outside Claiborne Pell's megalopolis? The nation, throwing out its railroads, was throwing out a century of investment. Henceforth, the cost of restoring it would be prohibitive. Europe had resolved not to make that decision, just as America had ceased to care.

Might not the railroads have united more creatively—indeed, less disruptively—to resolve their common problems? The railroads would say they did, by forming mergers to head off bankruptcy. Where history insists they failed was in their sweeping disdain for anything resembling intervention. They wanted the public out of the way. In the railroads' view, the public was synonymous with rules and regulations—with Big Government—and thus no friend.

Ultimately, the public simply walked away (or drove away). Airlines are now in a comparable situation. With their backs to the wall, airlines repeat the arrogance of the railroads: the public should be thankful there is any service. The railroads said it first. Why mention an obligation to the land or anything else? By the 1960s, it was as if their century of contributions to the arts, preservation, and industrial design had meant nothing at all. Today, few environmentalists and fewer railroad executives know the depth of their historical alliance, or realize that America the Beautiful once depended mightily on the work of both.

America continues to pay the price. If American railroads now seem to feel old, it has nothing to do with how they might have been. We can only imagine how the public's affection might have grown if they had honestly modernized. To do that, the railroads needed to keep their people base, a base including passengers. Without the passenger train, the railroads were on their own, no longer recognized—and no longer revered—as the principal carriers of the American dream.

chapter 5

Vows Made
to Rivers

The Indians had called the river Susquehanna. The word probably means "muddy river," although romanticists prefer "river of the winding shore." Certainly, the latter is the more colorful, spiritual reminder of the river *Phoebe Snow* and I called home.[1] My house was on Lookout Street, aptly named except for the surrounding trees. Then fall would come and with it, from my bedroom window, the restoration of Binghamton's railroads to sight and sound. The eastbound departure of the *Phoebe Snow* reminded me why railroads had married rivers. The rhythmic sound of her engines was unmistakable, even where the Binghamton skyline veiled the tracks. The moment it started and grew louder, I knew that *Phoebe* was pulling out. A few minutes later, she would be past the buildings and the giant gas tank, and would finally stretch full length into view. Now beside the water, she quickened the pace, momentarily to slip with the river behind the hills. Even out of sight, *Phoebe*'s cadence still told the story of a pathway smooth and delightfully effortless. As the resonance faded it reassured me: a gentle path was all a railroad needed. Where *Phoebe* resided, where railroads resided, the rivers of America ran undefiled.

As change descended across the valley, I welcomed *Phoebe*'s gentleness all the more. It was gargantuan change—superhighways—Interstate 81 and Route 17. Discounting critics, *Parade* magazine assured its Sunday readers that modern highways need not be excessive, then annually proved the assertion by recognizing one as the best designed. In short, a new highway should be aesthetically pleasing and uniquely respectful of its terrain. From the White House, Lady Bird Johnson added, "and free of billboards." There followed the Highway Beautification Act, passed in 1965. So there it was—*Parade*'s vision for the future confirmed by Congress and the president. The Interstate Highway System, although speeding commerce, would befriend the landscape no less than railroads.[2]

From my bedroom window I was not so sure. *Phoebe Snow* contented herself with a natural pathway, crossing the river, where necessary, on a kiss of steel. In contrast, the highways' earthmovers split apart entire hillsides, pushing the dirt into great embankments. Approaching the river, the highways stayed elevated on a forest of concrete pillars, then went airborne above the trees. Never had bridges seemed more excessive. And *Parade* was supporting *that*?

No, *Parade* was touting, as was Detroit, places where superhighways genuinely presented scenery—which most certainly was not here. What remained of the riverbank was an on-ramp—or was it an exit? Who could tell (and did it matter) was the point of stewardship. Another fishing hole was gone, another spot of redemption deep in the urban landscape. What had the engineers been thinking—or were they thinking? They had only to go 40 miles to observe Starrucca Viaduct, the Erie Railroad's great work of art. Now *that* had been a bridge, whose completion in 1848 had attracted painters of the Hudson River school.[3] I doubted anyone would be painting these bridges (I was wrong—they are constantly being covered with graffiti). But fine—Starrucca Viaduct, made of Pennsylvania blue stone, was probably too hard to replicate. Then why not a concrete bridge like Tunkhannock Viaduct, also an attraction for scores of artists and again, standing but 50 miles away. If superhighways were to be truly loved, was it not reasonable to expect some worthy architecture?

Highways were not about love, *Phoebe* reminded me. A bridge was meant as pure utility, to toss vehicles from side to side. Who needed artists to be painting that? Afterward, an exuberant river might still be muddy and elsewhere show its curve and grace. But any advantage the highway demanded—and big trucks especially demanded—the assaulted river must now obey.

A faith in rivers still required a faith in trains; history disagreed with *Parade*. Granted, working rivers and working trains had many rough marriages of their own. The steel mills and factories snaking the banks of eastern rivers were hardly inviting or picturesque. Pennsylvania's coal mines, leaking acid into the Susquehanna River, could depress anyone with their squalor. The Lackawanna Railroad, serving coal and steel, was

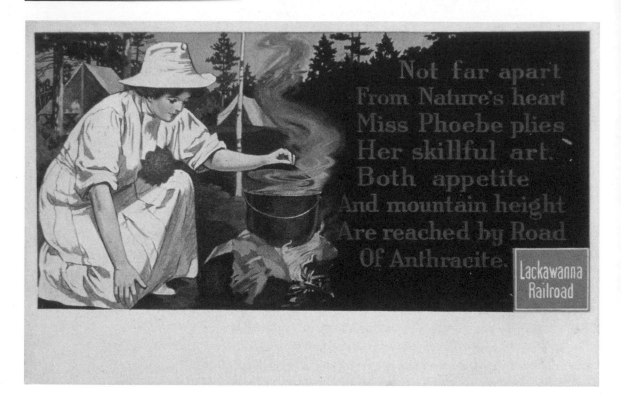

LACKAWANNA RAILROAD'S NEW STREAMLINER "THE PHOEBE SNOW" PASSING THROUGH
DELAWARE WATER GAP, PENNSYLVANIA

part of those landscapes too. The point about railroads remained their desire to concentrate industry, allowing industry to relent, as did the railroads. Now, with the coming of the superhighways, all of the Susquehanna Valley had been thrown open to development.

The railroads had required planning, and at the very least, made people agree on where they wished to live. A railroad was not about to go everywhere, offering interchanges by the score. The railroads had had limitations, some wanted and others ordained. Constructing railroads, engineers gladly bent with a river, refusing to break it out of spite. All along the riverbank, reconcilement might still be possible. At least a railroad might ask forgiveness in the certainty of returning trees. Superhighways mindlessly believed in straightness, even seeking to cut through city parks. What mattered was eminent domain and whether highway builders could obtain miles of right-of-way with just a single purchase. More than once, highways turned parks, forests, and wildlife refuges into corridors, brushing nature to the side.

Conservationists better aware of the contributions of railroads might have helped save the passenger train. Instead, their voice for railroads was barely audible as they concentrated on what was wild. American rivers, even if only "scenic," should recall the nation before the Fall. Railroads, as an industry, just had to be part of the slippage from wild to developed. Protecting rivers, conservationists lived for those memories of wilderness in the nineteenth century. Then names like Hudson, Potomac, Connecticut, and Delaware had conjured up great, unblemished landscapes. Rivers had been national icons. Ascending nearby cliffs and mountains, artists thrilled as they looked down at the rivers meandering through unbroken forests. It is no wonder that artists finally admitted their despair on canvas, watching, as settlements crept across the valleys, the ruination of their perfect Eden.[4]

Why could conservationists, admitting the reality of technology, not agree that railroads were protectors? If there had to be a technology, why not pick railroads instead of highways? But the railroads, turning negative, compromised the relationship by dumping passengers. Thus, by the 1960s, even conservationists had forgotten the good things railroads did,

Two *Phoebe Snow* postcards, thirty-five years apart, show the durability of landscape as an advertising theme. Above, Phoebe Snow camping out, ca. 1915. Below, the steamliner *Phoebe Snow* in the Delaware Water Gap, ca. 1950. Both author's collection.

East or west, a famous river was sure to invite a railroad to proclaim its respect for landscape. *Above,* from 1934, and *facing page,* from 1938, these route guides of the Chicago, Burlington & Quincy Railroad pledge that over hundreds of miles of railroad, nature still prevails. Both author's collection.

finally concluding that *all* industry was the enemy. In fact, losing wilderness to technology need not lead to ugliness, but that is what conservationists now believed.

Nor was it clear what they wanted, even among themselves. What was preservation, and conservation, and environmentalism? What aesthetic for the national landscape encompassed all these terms? Personally, I could live with rails snaked beside the Susquehanna if they allowed a passage as grand as the *Phoebe Snow*'s. I accepted the Lackawanna Railroad because it believed in the river too. The moment ballast crumbled away to riverbank, nature reclaimed the shore. It was not wilderness, but the trees and wildflowers were just as comforting, as if nothing commercial had interfered.

Of course, this was the railroad many years after construction, after time had allowed the landscape to heal. But railroads rarely changed their minds; finding the perfect route, they generally stuck with it, allowing its beauty to return. Engineering might still end in poetry. Sumac and willow were not the redwoods; goldenrod and aster were simple flowers, but they were beautiful and they healed the landscape. Is this not the greater imperative of conservation?

With highways, there remained too many temptations for starting over: another interchange, another industrial "park," another subdivision, another warehouse. Nor was the original construction sensitive to landscape: even decades after their completion, the embankments of superhighways still tumble, slip, and gully. Pounded constantly by heavy traffic, even the best-designed highways sound excessive. A train intrudes but a moment, then as rapidly turns a bend. It is as if the train had just dissolved. In that age of reason, of coexistence with landscape, the voice of the Susquehanna Valley was *Phoebe Snow*'s.

After her discontinuance, only two trains survived in the Susquehanna Valley, the *Lake Cities* and the *Owl*. Unfortunately, neither reminded us of what the *Phoebe*, a daylight train, had accomplished on behalf of landscape. Both sections of the *Lake Cities* entered New York State in the middle of the night. Aboard the *Owl*, everything in Pennsylvania, eastbound and westbound, was clothed in darkness the entire way.

To my surprise, this point surfaced in an article in *American Heritage* in December 1968. The magazine had decided to revisit the Lackawanna Railroad, featuring the legendary *Phoebe Snow*, but the bold type at the top suggested that the article would be a dirge: "'Bye, *Phoebe Snow,* / 'Bye, Buffalo. / What a way it was to go! / But if you'll travel home this Yule, / Eschew the Road of Diesel Fuel."[5] It seemed too soon for me to be looking back on anything; after all, I was only twenty-one.

Oliver Jensen, as senior editor, had obviously hoped for that response. What had happened to the railroad's pride? This was the route of Phoebe Snow, the legend behind every legend of the dawn of American advertising. How might the Phoebe used in the original ads feel today? Jensen asked. He sent his secretary off with a photographer to find out. She would retrace the route posing as the character Phoebe of the original series of ads, naturally wearing a gown of white. Cleverly, each photograph then appeared with a jingle intended to replicate the original Phoebe ads and postcards. Only for Jensen's Phoebe there would be obstacles, demanding that her jingles be entirely new.

At Hoboken station, the new Phoebe just about threw up. "What deep reproach! / (Was that a roach?) / There's just one single sit-up coach!" A final satirical barrage, noting her journey, indicated that she had missed the best scenery too. "O landscape bright, / O mountain height! / How can she see / Them in the night? / But dawn does come, / Toward Binghamton. / The passengers? / How many?—One."[6]

The railroads were winning, *American Heritage* confirmed, in their war against the passenger. As the Erie-Lackawanna had done with the *Phoebe Snow*, the railroads were picking on their best trains first. After *Phoebe*, no train in the Susquehanna Valley provided a daylight passage for viewing scenery, or a convenient time of arrival. Even a passenger train, if kept in the dark, could be reduced to pure utility.

American Heritage was onto something; I, too, was beginning to understand. Preservationists, now called environmentalists, no longer remembered railroads.[7] Why should the railroads not step aside and let American rivers "return to nature?" Established in 1968, the first system of wild and scenic rivers anticipated exactly that. Environmentalists begrudged anything technical that might interfere. Ideally, railroad rights-of-way would be abandoned, or at least realigned back from rivers. The very terms *wild* and *scenic* called for reducing "the built environment."[8]

It was a case of fewer trains teaching history, reminding environmentalists what had really displaced natural beauty. In the Susquehanna Valley, as all across America, environmentalists were about to confront the true displacers. Opposition to protected status for the Susquehanna

Following pages: J. Craig Thorpe, *Susquehanna River at Azilum, Pennsylvania*, 2005. Pen and ink, 15 x 22 inches. Collection of Deborah and Louis Steplock. Used by permission of the artist.

SUSQUEHANNA RIVER AT AZILUM, PENNSYLVANIA

River had coalesced around the U.S. Army Corps of Engineers. In the agency's "expert" view, the river and its upper tributaries required a series of 120 dams. For the sacrifice of 75,000 acres of farms and forests, the basin would gain stability—greater flood control, reduced sedimentation, and reliable stream flow in the summer months. Trust us, said the corps, to make the Susquehanna River safer and more inviting.[9]

Thus had *Phoebe*'s world—and mine—come face to face with the greater threat. Forget building a railroad alongside the riverbank; the corps was proposing a flood. Forget about terms like "wild" and "scenic"; the corps was proposing annihilation. Environmentalists unable to understand an accommodating technology were about to get one that accommodated nothing. Nowhere in the corps's reports was even a shred of *Phoebe*'s modesty. Here it comes—development—and after the dams, the power lines. And did we mention how all those reservoirs might cool a string of atomic power plants?

Now, if the *Phoebe Snow* ever did return, I worried whether it would be to a landscape still worth her greeting. Unconvinced, my friends and I grew determined to build our memories while the landscape we loved still survived. Our favorite route for day trips dipped us south into Pennsylvania, where, in the Endless Mountains, we rejoined the Susquehanna. We had gone 70 miles, the river twice that distance, arcing wide to the west and south. Here the river, now wide and majestic, looked grandly opposite to that of home. Again, the Army Corps of Engineers had promised us that no feature of the river was immutable, and shortly might not even be natural. But enough of that, we always agreed. Commiserating about the future would steal the day.

Without fail, we were drawn instinctively to our favorite overlooks, Azilum and Wyalusing Rocks. Along U.S. Highway 6, Azilum is the midpoint of a grand, three-sided arc in the river, with a broad valley inside the arc. It was to the lush fields and farms below that French anti-revolutionaries, in 1790, had hoped to spirit Marie Antoinette. Somehow, the meandering river enclosing the site seemed to mourn her loss, the guillotine having claimed her head. Satisfied that the corps had not yet beheaded the valley, we continued 5 miles east to Wyalusing Rocks. Perched 500 feet above the river, the cliffs drop precipitously to another breathtaking landscape, now recalling the American Revolution. In 1779, the Continental Army passed these cliffs, ascending the river to rendezvous with a second force floating down from Otsego Lake (the site of Cooperstown, New York, and the source of the Susquehanna). United, the army fought a sharp battle at Newtown (near Elmira), then burned a swath across the Finger Lakes region, targeting dozens of Iroquois villages whose warriors had aided or allied with British troops.

After rereading the historical markers, we savored again the gorgeous views, a mosaic of fields and farmhouses dispersing against foothills and a deepening forest. Farthest against the horizon, the flattened ridges of the Endless Mountains veiled our hiking destination for the day. Both overlooks came with a row of cabins set back modestly among the trees. Rustic cottages provided meals and souvenirs, and thus remained, in the historical view of preservation, both tasteful and legitimate. In exchange for providing tourists a small advantage, each lent incentive to protect the overlooks, ensuring that Azilum and Wyalusing would forever remain (or so we hoped) protected against vandalism and graffiti.

In retrospect, however, the primary steward was still below, where it taught the reciprocity now in jeopardy everywhere. Close to the river ran that steward—the historic Lehigh Valley Railroad. Competing with the Erie and Lackawanna railroads, it too had claimed portions of the Susquehanna River for gentle grades. But the tracks remained barely noticeable, thanks again to the encroaching trees. Still, the greater point was that the railroad reached high into the mountains, finding the overlooks and wanting them whole. Not just the river, but the cliffs and hills adorning it should remain what the railroad called the Switzerland of America.

On days when the distant mountains were boiling thunderheads, they seemed indeed to touch the sky. No matter—watching the trains come and go (now all freight), we allowed the Lehigh Valley Railroad its hyperbole. Certainly, the river did not seem to mind. Whether upstream beside the Erie-Lackawanna, or here, where the Lehigh Valley made its entrance, always that ribbon of trees betokened tranquility rather than estrangement or disrespect.

By evening we had returned, hoping for a sunset up to the magic of the last. We seemed never to be disappointed. A deepening band of colors above Azilum promised perfection at Wyalusing Rocks. At Azilum the river is slightly distant; at Wyalusing it is almost directly below the cliffs. "Sky water," Henry David Thoreau reminded us in *Walden,* "It needs no fence."[10] Gloriously, there were no fences here, just that brilliant sweep of water advancing beneath our feet, tossing the twilight across its ripples in deepening bursts of gold and red.

One of those special sunsets, my friend Brad reminds me, was in the summer of 1968. "You remember that evening," he still insists. "The sunset lingered as you, I, Joanne, and Barbara sat on the slope above Azilum. The whole sky was bathed in pink. Suddenly, there was a flickering in the distance—a headlight!—and in unison we shouted 'Train!' Still at the far side of the valley, already in darkness, the engines seemed to be barely moving. Then the breeze floated the whistle up to us, followed by the rumbling of the wheels. It took forever to pass beneath the overlook, so

SUSQUEHANNA RIVER AT WYALUSING ROCKS, PENNSYLVANIA

great is the river's arc. We kept watching it curve away, its headlight dusting the trees and cliffs. Not until the caboose had slipped behind the mountain did you suggest we leave to watch moonrise at Wyalusing."

How could I not remember? The humidity drawing the river to our nostrils and the added fragrance of our grassy perch, the "Summer of our Youth," he calls it, and fall still far away.

But fall did come, and Brad found himself in the army. College over, youth behind him, the next year he was headed for Vietnam. There he drew combat duty in a rifle company, meaning struggling to survive fire fights. Then it happened—he was hit, his column struck by a mortar attack. Men and vehicles sped in all directions, everyone trying to escape the shells. One moment Brad was running, and suddenly he was down. But it was not a bullet or a shell; a jeep had hit him from behind. In another instant a truck was on top of him, crushing him into the mud. Worse, the truck was a flatbed, and carried a bulldozer. Brad felt his ribs give way, and his organs, before the wheels finally released their grip. Only the mud had saved him. But his buddies, lifting him onto a stretcher, knew he would die. So did the nurses meeting the wounded as his chopper landed at Lon Binh.

At Lon Binh hospital, in the Green Room, Brad realized he had been put in triage. The seven men lying to either side of him were expected to die as well. For the next several hours, he sensed only the doctors and nurses moving about, whispering, "This one is gone...this one too." Then the orderlies would arrive, making other sounds, as they struggled each corpse into a body bag. One orderly would grab the zipper as another pulled tight the folds. *Bizzip*!!! Brad had never found the sound of a zipper so terrifying. He needed desperately to think of some other sound if he were to live through triage and see the morning.

But what sound could that possibly be? Then it came to him—Azilum. He imagined himself back on the bluff. It was summer again, there was the river, all of us gazing into the distance shouting "Train!" Hear it, then! Live for it! Shut those goddamned zippers out! Miracles do happen, we are told to believe. Brad believes. After all, the only body bag unfilled in the morning was the one that had been meant for him.

J. Craig Thorpe, *Susquehanna River at Wyalusing Rocks, Pennsylvania*, 2005. Pen and ink, 15 x 22 inches. Collection of Deborah and Louis Steplock. Used by permission of the artist.

After that worst night of his life, there were still many bad nights ahead. Each time, he asked Azilum to get him through. It did. There remained the plane ride to Tokyo, the surgeries, and the endless months of convalescing in the states. Still the river never left his side. When finally we were reunited, back in Binghamton, he was planning his marriage to Joanne.

Landscape need not be wilderness to be inspiring. That is the lesson here. For me, the proof had been the *Phoebe Snow;* for Brad, the whistle of a common freight train. As witnesses to a vanishing wilderness, artists and writers of the nineteenth century had hoped as much. America the Wild might become America the Beautiful, but America should not accept any less.

Pursuing beauty, if not agreeing to wilderness, the railroads had done their part. Which is how Brad and I, exploring the Susquehanna River, had come to agree with history. A railroad running next to our river seemed just fine with us. It still does. After all, we have that summer evening, blessed with a train and a river, when Brad saw the beauty in both that would save his life.

The Debate
We Never Had

Ideally, the United States in the 1960s could have seriously debated the future of its railroads. Instead, crises dominated the national press; watershed events included the civil rights movement and the war in Vietnam. Four national leaders were struck down by assassins: John F. Kennedy (1963), Malcolm X (1965), Robert F. Kennedy (1968), and Martin Luther King (1968). Even if the press had wanted to cover railroad issues, each tragedy invited only a looking back. President Kennedy's assassination reinforced the comparisons between Kennedy and Abraham Lincoln, as the nation remembered the image of Lincoln's funeral train. Once again, negative symbolism confirmed the notion that railroads were a thing of the past.

Five years later, Senator Robert Kennedy's funeral sealed this image. After the ceremony at St. Patrick's Cathedral in New York, his body went to Washington DC—by train. Hundreds of thousands of mourners lined the tracks. As the family and the press explained, Senator Kennedy had been in love with trains. Yet another fateful symbolism suggested that trains were a dying way of life.

The point about a period of national tragedy is that everything else comes to be weighed against it. Undoubtedly, if the 1960s had ended as they began—in peace and unparalleled prosperity—debating railroads would not have seemed irrelevant. Instead, Vietnam obsessed the nation;

effectively, the war was our only priority. What congressional attention the railroads did receive was due largely to the support of Senator Claiborne Pell of Rhode Island. It appeared there would be high-speed trains in the Northeast under the High-Speed Ground Transportation Act of 1965, and Congress appropriated $90 million for the demonstration project.[1] Everywhere else, as the nation slipped into social overload, it seemed that trains would disappear.

Like the national debate on the war in Vietnam, the debate on railroads was about life and death; people were just loath to admit the similarities. In the 1960s, highway fatalities averaged 50,000 per year. Between 1963 and 1973, 58,000 Americans were killed in Vietnam—certainly a tragic number. But in 1973 alone, an equal number of people were killed on the nation's highways, and in the ten years between 1963 and 1973, the death toll on America's highways totaled 500,000.[2]

There is no Memorial Day or Veterans Day to honor those killed in cars. Everyone knows the difference between a highway and a battlefield, but it is our cultural habit—cultural convenience—to separate death into categories. Obviously, there is a difference, but our denial is disturbing. If the Vietnam War was considered a national tragedy because 58,000 died on battlefields, why did Americans not challenge the 500,000 deaths on highways as equally tragic and equally wasteful?

Of course, some did, but never in a way to suggest that America should rethink traveling by car. Rather, the government should make it safer. The irony remains in the risks Americans accept for the privilege of using highways. Who would tolerate that level of risk on *public* transport? The crash of an airplane unnerves us all: My God, I could have been on that flight! Immediately, the federal government leaps into action, ordering investigators to the scene. On site, specialists sift through the smallest bits of evidence and, if possible, reassemble the entire plane. Next come the interminable hearings, expert testimony, and follow-up directives to the airlines. Just as quickly, a battery of lawyers assembles to represent the victims' families. In the end, everyone accuses the government as much as the airline of not anticipating the problem. If the airplane had been better designed or better maintained, it would not have crashed in the first place. Boarding an airplane, we expect perfection; entering a car, we do not even think to check the tires.

The double standard is amazing when we stop to think of the body count. Every day, the equivalent of a 737 crashes on the nation's streets and highways. The silence of the outcry is deafening because the crash site is so huge. The tragedy is just as real; it is simply scattered across the country. Car by car and body by body, the crash site forms incrementally throughout the day. There is no fireball, no big explosion that the press can see and dramatize. A car accident has to have many fatalities or be a gargantuan pileup even to be reported nationally. Yet if the National Transportation Safety Board cannot determine the cause of a single plane crash, the whole nation is afraid to fly.

The debate America sidestepped in the 1960s might have begun by acknowledging the inconsistency. Since then, the automobile has claimed another 1.5 million lives. Dead on the highways, they are One Big Accident—evidence not of the nation's lack of choice (or responsibility), but rather of the assumption that driving is about tempting fate.

In such a climate of national acceptance, the passenger train lost its last, defining argument. Granted, the railroads had their own periods of abysmal safety, especially when coaches and Pullman cars were made of wood. Hundreds died, and in some years thousands, spread among wrecks and crossing accidents. Hundreds more died as laborers. A century ago, all railroad deaths, from all causes, averaged 10,000 annually.[3] That was still but a fifth of the fatalities from the worst years for auto accidents, and less than a fourth of the auto fatalities now.[4] Moreover, once Congress mandated safety features for the railroads, their fatalities dropped dramatically. When it comes to safety, it is the automobile, not the train or airplane, that government has let off the hook.

Face it, the moment anyone challenges the automobile, our cultural knee-jerk reaction is to make excuses: one could just as easily slip in the bathtub or fall down a flight of stairs. It is not that the car is innately more dangerous, but rather that people travel by car so much. Given the enormity of the pool of risk-takers, inevitably, a larger percentage will have to die. Of course, we expect it to be the other guy. If running the system demands a victim, let it be someone else.

No amount of denial or statistical shadow boxing can hide the awful truth. Only the car threatens every one of us with the possibility of death so often in a single lifetime.[5] Only the car has killed more than 50,000 Americans in any single year, and more than 3 million people in the twentieth century. With less than half that number (1.265 million) dead on battlefields, all the wars ever fought by the United States do not even come close.[6]

The automobile is a tragedy impossible to assess if no one will consider it a tragedy. So long as death comes as a statistic—one we believe will fall on someone else—few Americans are likely to be convinced that the price of the automobile has grown too steep.

In the debate we never had, the railroads might have turned those statistics to their advantage. The public chastises the railroads for cutting trains, yet admits its preference is the automobile. Since Americans so easily forgive the car for killing them, how can the passenger train compete?

The point is that the argument would have been disingenuous. The railroads themselves were in the process of slipping their own safety issues past the government. They intended to downsize by reducing tracks and maintenance, all the while introducing heavier and more dangerous loads. In truth, the railroads were pleased not to mention the passenger train at all.

Here is where the government, if not otherwise distracted, might have forestalled the railroads' downsizing and dismemberment. Dear Railroads: We cannot afford to rebuild you. We need you to preserve double track and keep up your maintenance, for which we would be pleased to forgive the appropriate taxes. In exchange for your keeping mail and passenger service, we will capitalize those costs for you. It never happened, the journalist Peter Lyon maintained, because the railroads never wanted it. After 1950, in two instances out of every three, the railroads themselves asked that the mail be dropped. Why? According to Lyon, it was so they could blame the government for forcing the discontinuance of the affected trains.[7]

Even if we discount the possibility of a conspiracy, the railroads' behavior says it all. Convinced that passengers were not its future, the industry tried everything to be rid of them. Granted, it did not happen all at once or happen uniformly. A few railroads believed in passengers until the end. But it is where the nation was heading; government knew it and did little to head it off.

Congress could have insisted the railroads were public utilities and not just a private enterprise. Railroads could have been reminded of the obligations included with the right to make a profit. Once government failed its obligations, the railroads could not help failing theirs as well. Critically, in the 1960s, the war in Vietnam had intervened. Stridency held the reins of culture. In every debate, government was singled out as the problem rather than the common protector of the nation's interests.

The political process lacked for trust. Railroads, holding to the political right, believed they owed the nation nothing. Each paid taxes on its entire right-of way, buildings and land included. That was more than enough. Passenger activists, tending to the political left, believed the railroads owed the nation everything. Had Congress forgotten all those land grants? And what about the sweetheart contracts during World War II? Only an informed, undistracted Congress could have arbitrated those differences fairly. It never happened in a climate of war, assassination, and cultural unrest.

Inevitably, efforts to determine how many passenger trains the nation needed succumbed to the question of whether we needed any at all. Worse, with attitudes toward the railroads becoming overwhelmingly negative, railroad history too became a weapon. Americans recalled the period when railroads thought of little but themselves. It was too easy to remember the bad things—the workers crushed to death while coupling boxcars with protruding hooks and pins, or tossed off a lurching train while setting its brakes by hand. Eventually, knuckle couplers and air brakes saved hundreds, even thousands, of lives per year, but not without resistance from the railroads, who considered labor expendable.

As well, every GI squeezed aboard a World War II troop train had a horror story of his own to tell. During the war, the railroads had pressed every car into service—equipment that, were it not for the Great Depression, would have been scrapped years before. Although by then there were modern trains, many with air conditioning, few GIs were offered those. Theirs came hot in summer and cold in winter and without enough seats or working toilets. Obviously the soldiers believed they were victims. It seemed, recalling history, that railroads still profited at the expense of the public, now abusing them as they had abused laborers.

Because millions had been affected, the consequences proved enormous. After the war, many ex-servicemen (and servicewomen) vowed never to ride a train again. Well into the 1980s, I was still meeting them and listening to them confess their distrust of trains. Finally, having not been on a train in forty years, they had decided to give Amtrak a try. In 1996, two veterans of George Patton's Third Army did the same, although their train, the luxurious *American Orient Express,* was hardly like riding Amtrak's standard fare. Regardless, their response fit all the others: "With our savings from the war, we bought a car as soon as possible. All of our buddies did. None of us wanted anything more to do with railroads, neither their rudeness nor their discomfort."

More than numbers and statistics, it is those common national experiences that define the boundaries of social change. Think how much the troop trains of the 1940s affected the passenger trains of the 1950s. Discount for the moment the exaggerated claim that cars were purchased to avoid the railroads. The GIs would have bought those cars no matter what. However, without their bad memories, ex-GIs might not have abandoned the railroads entirely and instead, by returning to trains just once in the 1950s (now with their families, too), might have helped swell passenger counts by the millions. Millions fewer Americans would have believed the passenger train was outdated. By the 1960s, it was too late.

In the West, the success of the vista dome, whose glass-enclosed, upper-level seating offered spectacular views, hinted to the industry what the era might have been. After the war, the most successful railroads were in the West, where, continually mindful of their scenery, most still believed in passengers. Inaugurated in 1949, the *California Zephyr* made

After World War II, air-conditioned dome cars attracted new passengers to railroads, especially in the West. Unfortunately, GIs painfully familiar with older troop trains were rarely among those passengers. In this 1955 ad, the Great Northern Railway announces full-length domes for the *Empire Builder*. Author's collection.

land cruising an instant hit. No airplane had a vista dome offering a 360-degree view of the passing landscape. The *California Zephyr* had five such cars.[8] By the mid-1950s, all the western carriers had them; following the *Zephyr*, the trains were timed to traverse their best scenery in daylight hours.[9] In 1971 Amtrak itself inherited its best equipment from the West. The railroads there had the all the advantages, serving an enviable base of natural resources, dramatic scenery, and long-distance freight and passenger services.

Ultimately, however, uncertainty dogged even the West. After all, passengers traveling east of Chicago were forced onto those weakening links. As more eastern routes dropped key trains, connections with the West were severed. What passenger, traveling across the continent, looked forward to declining trains half the way? The West was beautiful but not *that* beautiful. The more the railroads east of Chicago turned against the public, the more those in the West also paid the price.

The point remains that the United States might have resolved the issue if not so distracted by war and history. Government and the railroads might have educated the American public had they agreed on a common cause. Surely the public would agree that highways should not go everywhere and, accepting that, would agree to maintain the nation's railroads. Instead, too many suspicions (many of them historical) drained the railroads of their last support. As a rule, Americans preferred not to invest in an industry they believed would turn on them again.

Ultimately, the railroads, cornered by their history, tragically picked the wrong way out, abandoning the elegance of "welcome aboard" for "the public-be-damned." The suspicions of the traveling public were thus hardened and reconfirmed. After all, it was the railroads who had taught the public to equate the passenger train with corporate pride. And now it was the railroads who were undercutting that pride by insisting on limitations. In their haste to be rid of the passenger train, the railroads had dared to rattle every skeleton in the national closet, every lingering suspicion that corporations, left to themselves, would ignore the common good.

Just as the railroads had grown short on leadership, the government had grown short on time. The future of the passenger train could not possibly matter, weighed against the nation's chief concerns. Vietnam continued to sap the nation of its willingness to argue and reflect. The only hope was that enough routes could be saved from which the system might grow again. And so, in the debate over the future of the railroads, limiting routes and services was the only solution such troubled times would allow.

chapter 7

The Quick Fix

By the end of the 1960s, the passenger train was barely hanging on. Time and again, the railroads successfully painted it as a last gasp of pure nostalgia. Occasionally, the Interstate Commerce Commission disagreed, ordering that a train not be discontinued. The petitioning railroad had only to wait a few months, petition again, and generally the discontinuance was allowed. In Binghamton, consumer activists decried the pattern, last accusing the Erie-Lackawanna of assigning other costs to its passenger trains. Although the station housed freight and passenger offices, the railroad allegedly considered it just for passengers. So activists were convinced the Erie-Lackawanna had charged that station entirely to the *Phoebe Snow*. As it stood, her last reported loss (in 1965) was $93,940.[1] Adjusted for inflation, that would be serious today, but hardly catastrophic. What was going on?

The truth was hidden behind accounting practices that even the railroads could not explain.[2] At face value, it seemed logical to accept that passenger trains had to be losing money. Why would the railroads drop them otherwise? In that vein, the second installment in the railroads' argument sounded more convincing than the first. Their return on freight, they added, was nothing they could brag about. Technically, their capital would draw more in a bank. Passenger advocates were talking nonsense. It would be better if stockholders forgot about railroading altogether and ordered the directors to do something else. In fact, some of the largest railroads did just that, engaging in mergers and acquisitions of properties they knew little or nothing about.[3]

No airline was about to argue, nor would the combination of construction companies, engineers, and lobbyists joined in lockstep with the nation's highways. If the railroads welcomed losing business, all the better for their competitors.

Meanwhile, there were no major conferences, no significant arm-twisting, no demands that the railroads prove their claims.[4] Specifically, how would eliminating the passenger train help the freight train if the railroads, as they continued to argue, were barely making money either way?

Essentially, the debate was over before it started. Residual affection for the passenger train, Congress agreed, merited a skeletal national system, with trains that would finally be subsidized. It was a deal, then. Any railroad choosing not to join the system must agree to operate its remaining passenger trains. Only four decided to do so: the Southern, the Rock Island, the Denver & Rio Grande Western, and the Georgia railroads. On May 1, 1971, the rest transferred approximately four hundred passenger trains to the new National Railroad Passenger Corporation. Within hours, the new corporation (Amtrak for short) had slashed those remaining trains by half.[5]

The problem with hesitant, mediocre beginnings is ever getting past them. Every institution begins by developing a culture, one that is idealistic or expedient or something in between. Amtrak had no incentive to believe in brilliance. Fiscal absurdity dogged it from day one with an initial operating subsidy pegged at $40 million.[6] The railroads, now positioned as landlords leasing tracks to Amtrak, drained that in a flash. A second premise was just as ominous—the assumption that the nation could be served with single trains. But what if consumer activists had been right? What if the lack of trains indeed explained the lack of passengers and not the other way around?

Under the railroads, bleeding operations down to single trains had been the principal strategy of discontinuance. In Binghamton, that surviving train in the middle of the night ensured the death of would-be patronage in the afternoon. Amtrak could hardly hope to restore public confidence by resorting to the same level of inflexibility. The company would continue to serve major cities and important towns at inconvenient hours. Meanwhile expenses for all stations, maintenance, and personnel would have to be charged against those single trains.

The game was rigged. Rather than creating a blueprint for the future of rail transportation, Amtrak was to rationalize the railroads' argument that the nation did not need passenger trains. Now Amtrak itself was soaking up the argument, forging a culture that ignored common sense. We are giving you a train—what more could you possibly want?

Admittedly, Amtrak's inheritance was in shambles. There were not enough cars and locomotives, and too few of those in working order. That part the critics forgave. What critics could not understand is how often Amtrak sounded just like the railroads, and that is the point—it was. Along with their cars and locomotives, Amtrak had inherited many of the railroads' management personnel. Just days, weeks, or months before, those same people had been in charge of eliminating rail passenger service. Did a transfer to Amtrak make any difference? Had they recanted the 1960s, checking their prejudices at the door?

My experience as a director of the National Association of Railroad Passengers (1974–82) consistently told me "no." Divided allegiances were rife in Amtrak. Executives openly confessed that if Amtrak got the ax, they expected to return "home" to their former railroads, which had turned to freight service alone. Merely to hold out that possibility discouraged Amtrak executives from taking any risks. Rather, their attitude focused on appeasing their former employers: what did the "home" railroad want them to do? As it stood, those railroads ran the trains, advanced the crews, and supplied every mile of track. If and when those operations fully shifted to Amtrak, how would the new company have a mind of its own?

In 1976 a first transfer allowed Amtrak to purchase the Northeast Corridor; finally, in the 1980s, Amtrak crews began running its national trains. But to this day, everything outside the Northeast Corridor is leased. No matter who runs the trains, Amtrak remains a ward of the railroads.

Certainly, the railroads had not changed their minds. Whether their trains or Amtrak's trains, they believed the passenger train should go. Never had I heard the prejudice expressed as openly as in 1974 when invited to address a San Francisco program of the National Railway Historical Society, I shared my presentation with a senior vice president of the Southern Pacific Railroad. Turning to me on the dais, he introduced himself as the "young Turk," who, twenty years before, had convinced the Southern Pacific to phase out its passenger trains. How? By not purchasing any new equipment but making do with the cars it had. Then, when those cars were shot, the railroad could drop its passenger trains.

Now Amtrak was his target. It was just ludicrous, he began his speech, to save the passenger train. The Southern Pacific Railroad needed to be free of passengers, and other railroads should follow suit. Freight trains were growing longer, up to two hundred cars in length, with added engines in the middle and rear. Even with the extra engines, slow going in the mountains was inevitable. Congress should consider the difficulty of crossing Donner Pass in the Sierra Nevada with Amtrak "always in the way." Congress should get Amtrak's passenger trains out of the way. Next the unions would have to budge. Trains monitored and controlled electronically required only one man in the cab. Soon even he would be replaced, accruing bigger savings for the railroad. The final "advance" making that possible would be a computer capable of running everything.

Only someone ignorant of railroad history could possibly believe that Amtrak controlled its destiny. As long as the railroads were Amtrak's landlords, they would stand in Amtrak's way. Nothing had changed from the 1960s. The railroads considered passengers and laborers expendable, so Amtrak would be corroded from within. In the 1960s, the railroads had insisted their passengers could switch to buses or planes. Now those same executives, controlling Amtrak, complained about holdout passengers, including seniors, workers with passes, or people afraid to fly: they were all freeloaders on the taxpayers. The subliminal accusation was just as damaging: only people who were too cheap, too scared, or too old still wanted the long-distance passenger train.

Thus Amtrak, pursuing the public in one sector, insulted the public in every other. Worse, Amtrak's attitude ran counter to its own stated purpose: to give all Americans the choice they deserved. No one anywhere should be forced to travel feeling intimidated or afraid; no one should have to apologize for taking trains. But there was Amtrak, like the railroads, asking the customer to apologize for daring to suggest what service meant.[7]

The interpretation is inescapable: the passenger train had survived the 1970s purely on the strength of past affection. Enough loyalty survived from the 1950s for the nation not to give up on Amtrak. Enough Americans demanded that Congress and the railroads not drop the experiment of a national rail passenger system.[8]

It helped that activists, noting that Congress was watching, took every opportunity to ride and raise the numbers. Then a doctoral student and lecturer at the University of California–Santa Barbara, I considered my opportunity—riding to San Francisco—heaven on earth. It was amazing to consider that this scenic gem had been an afterthought, an eleventh-hour addition to the national system. Released November 30, 1970, by the U.S. Department of Transportation, the original system map had called for east–west trains terminating in Seattle, San Francisco, and Los Angeles. None of those cities was to be linked north to south. More ominously, a counterproposal from the White House suggested just a single western train, perhaps splitting in Salt Lake City.[9]

Aided by the Interstate Commerce Commission, rail passenger advocates saved the day. The final agreement was as ordained. Three separate trains would depart Chicago for Seattle, San Francisco, and Los Angeles. Another train, terminating in Los Angeles, would depart from New Orleans. And yes, the historic Coast Route of the Southern Pacific Railroad would be retained to connect them all. The route's only drawback would be frequency. Initially, only the California portion, between Los Angeles and San Francisco, would have daily trains. From San Francisco (actually Oakland), the train would continue north just three times a week, then, returning south from Seattle and Portland, operate on the same schedule to Los Angeles.

The point is that the entire route—what would emerge as Amtrak's single most popular train—was not even considered at the outset. Activists (and the ICC) protested the absurdity of not connecting cities with millions of residents. The route included the West Coast's major colleges and universities in cities large and small. Scenic diversity sealed the route's excitement, highlighted by a progression of tidelands, bays, valleys, mountain ranges, and beaming volcanic peaks.

Indeed, for many riders (myself included), it was the scenery that made this train incredible, with 110 miles of the route hugging the rugged Pacific coast. Northbound, the ocean is visible approaching Oxnard, California; southbound, after leaving San Luis Obispo, the train pierces a cleft in the coastal range. Today there are many troubling changes in the landscape, including new subdivisions and upscale homes; however, throughout the 1970s, it remained a countryside reminiscent of Old California. Leaving the suburbs of Los Angeles, lemon and orange groves lined the tracks. Between Gaviota and Vandenberg Air Force Base, two major ranches, covering thousands of acres, spilled cattle high into the hills. But it was the ocean that took my breath away, the tracks often clinging to precipitous cliffs, with breakers crashing against the rocks below as the train carefully returned to level ground.

How could anyone have thought for a moment this train should not be part of Amtrak? Now management, too, seemed chagrined. How was Amtrak (and the Southern Pacific Railroad) to explain the success of a long-distance train? It was not supposed to happen that way. But the *Coast Starlight* continually filled up with passengers, surpassing 500 on many runs. The sleeping cars, too, were selling out, depriving me of a favorite upgrade—a roomette for the day. After 1972, I never rode a train carrying fewer than 250 passengers and once, in June 1976, the conductor informed me 600 were on board.

Any airline would have been ecstatic to fill a 747 every day. Moreover, after June 1973, when the *Coast Starlight* went daily, Amtrak found itself

The *Coast Starlight*, originally left out of the Amtrak system, is shown at Gaviota, California, in June 1975. The train's name remains something of a misnomer since both sections, northbound and southbound, traverse the actual coast in daylight. Photograph by the author.

filling four sections (the number needed to serve the entire route). However, daily service had come grudgingly. Disclosing its internal prejudice, Amtrak discounted the *Starlight*'s figures, observing that only 3 percent of passengers rode from end to end. Amtrak argued that there was no need for a long-distance train—the 97 percent of passengers who were riding a shorter distance could just as easily be served by corridors, and the remaining 3 percent could fly. The point remained that the *Starlight* was an embarrassment to managers convinced the future of Amtrak was in city pairs of their choosing.

Amtrak headquarters wanted its passengers to fit a mold, but the mold was refusing to fit. After all, a train is not an airplane and while covering 1,400 miles will exchange a good number of passengers along the way. The more revealing (and reasonable) comparison was region-to-region travel, in which case Amtrak's absurdity was indisputable. Forty percent of patrons were traveling 1,000 miles or more; for example, getting on at Tacoma just south of Seattle and, if not going all the way to Los Angeles, stopping just short at Santa Barbara. Why did Amtrak assume that every passenger had to go end-to-end to be legitimate? No railroad had ever thought that way before. The point was filling seats, not insulting passengers for wanting choices. If filled for the entire 1,400 miles, the seat itself had gone the distance. On average, two and one-third passengers were using that seat, an impressive commitment of 600 miles per patron.[10]

Ultimately, Amtrak was just proving how much the railroads still influenced policy. The success of the *Starlight* proved that the Southern Pacific Railroad had earlier schemed against its passengers. What was Amtrak's purpose in criticizing the *Starlight* if not hoping similarly to discontinue the train? Amtrak's latest mantra all but admitted it. The so-called legitimate trains were the corridor trains, those moving business travelers and commuters.

Then was travel for pleasure illegitimate? Amtrak's first orders for new equipment emphatically said yes. Windows were smaller, seats closer together, and dining and lounge cars virtually absent. Fast food was in, prepared food out. Henceforth, every seat-back would come with a tray table, just like on the airlines. The so-called lounge car was just for ordering. From there, passengers carried their food back to the coaches, clutched in a cardboard box. Inside were plastic dishes and plastic forks, all of it going out with the garbage. Since Amtrak intended passengers to travel short distances, it was unreasonable that they should ask for more.[11]

The railroads also wanted these changes—if Amtrak ever became something special, it would disprove the railroads' argument. And there it was in the *Starlight*—visible proof that the railroads had deserted the public as much as the public had deserted them. Not every train in America had deserved discontinuance; rather, the railroads had simply wanted out.

Certainly, the treatment Amtrak itself was giving the Coast Route spoke volumes about the history. In my approximately one hundred days aboard the *Starlight*, only a third of the trains performed as advertised. My apartment beside the tracks in Santa Barbara allowed me to check on the progress of many others. It seemed the trains were never on time. But aboard the trains it was worse: rarely were the restrooms clean, the windows clean, or the chair car attendants present to carry suitcases. In some cars, the glass (now commonly plastic) had so deteriorated that it was opaque. Even from the dome, the brilliance of the day was generally lost because the windows gave the appearance of traveling through a fog.

The point is that when the train worked properly, the *Coast Starlight* was a gem. Railroad supporters kept the faith in the hope of repeating so incredible a journey, betting that the *Starlight* would live up to the magnificence of its coastal passage one more time. Ultimately, the *Starlight* proved the salvation of Amtrak nationwide. Despite management and despite the railroads, the word kept getting out: trains could still be fun and inspiring. America the Beautiful was worth the effort. Maybe, just maybe, Amtrak had a future, after all.

Unfortunately, the railroads still had other ideas, and now tried a different tack. Even those single passenger trains, they began accusing Amtrak, were disproportionately in the way of the railroads' freight trains. If Amtrak wanted its trains to run on time, it should be willing to pay a premium. The initial contract had been but an installment—money down just for use of the tracks. On-time performance was an added "burden" for which an "incentive" should be paid.

As a corporate strategy, incentives were closer to extortion. First, the city of termination determined the incentive; only the last stop need be "on time." This led to a major flimflam—padding the schedule for those last few miles. In a final sleight of hand, the railroads demanded that the published schedule be ignored. The railroads insisted upon (and got) a grace period of thirty minutes for on-time performance.

A press more attuned to the railroads' shenanigans might have reported the practice openly. How could the *Starlight*, running ninety minutes late into Santa Barbara, be on time when it arrived in Los Angeles? That was just 100 miles away. How could the Southern Pacific Railroad even pretend it had run the train on time for the entire route? What allowed the railroads to ask for thousands of dollars extra to guarantee on-time performance for just one city?[17] If the long-distance passenger train had not been a money loser before, it most certainly was now.

As always, the press preferred the obvious stories, coaxing the passengers to give up sound bites. It was much easier to write trip reports than to convince Amtrak executives to come clean. Discrepancies hidden deep in the culture of railroads required investigative skills. The press preferred entertaining with simple stories rather than working to reveal the complex facts.

Amtrak's negatives continued to outweigh its positives. Reflecting its beginnings, it consistently lowered expectations. Fundamentally, Amtrak believed in decreasing rail passenger service to the bare minimum, and finally (just as the railroads wanted) dropping the passenger train virtually everywhere. Locked into a minimum level of performance, any culture can learn to embrace it. Worse yet, there remained the possibility that

Amtrak would believe in its own mediocrity enough to demand that critics call it excellence.

Whatever happened, the uninformed public would blame Amtrak and not the railroads. There the railroads had obviously won by creating in the public mind (as they had in Congress) a separation that did not exist. The logic of this thinking was just as faulty as a car owner blaming the manufacturer for a bumpy road. Amtrak could do only so much against the animosity of the people who owned the roads. The nation needed reform throughout the entire railroad system—not just within Amtrak. To be sure, that day has still not arrived.

Tunnel Vision

Throughout Amtrak's evolution, many would compare the historical, continental vision of railroads to Amtrak's more limited version. In most of the United States, there tended to be a single train departing every day, but sometimes only three times a week. Only the Northeast Corridor, Amtrak alleged, possessed the prerequisites for round-the-clock, hourly service. Here were half a dozen major cities anchored by New York, and the space between those cities was filling in. With 40 million residents—still one-fifth of the entire country's population in 1971—the Northeast Corridor was closest to the European model. In theory, because a corridor tended to have a greater population density, it would also have a greater number of riders.

Everything else a train had been—a relationship with landscape, a reaffirmation of community—Amtrak either downplayed or ignored. The passenger train had been politicized far more than rediscovered. The nine states of the Northeast Corridor—Virginia, Maryland, Pennsylvania, Delaware, New Jersey, New York, Connecticut, Rhode Island, and Massachusetts—were represented by eighteen U.S. senators and 100 representatives (out of the 435 in the House of Representatives). This was not the place, Amtrak concluded, to be arguing for landscape over utility. Rather, the point of retaining the Northeast Corridor was the proximity of one financial market to another; its trains would carry stockbrokers, accountants, lawyers, and chairmen of the board. What Congress should subsidize, Amtrak agreed, was the "serious business traveler."

Critically, even Congress discounted the fact that cities in the Northeast Corridor were losing population to the suburbs. By the 1970s, the American city had many hearts. Just because Amtrak stopped in downtown New York or Philadelphia did not automatically mean millions of added customers—the business market had likely moved miles away, and the now-suburban managers and executives had no intention of backtracking just to ride a train.

The Northeast Corridor deserved to be developed and remained the nation's showpiece; however, Amtrak failed to acknowledge that the Corridor had problems of its own. The suburbs now hugged roads, not railroads. Those suburbs had developed as blobs, not lines. How would Amtrak get control of those blobs and shift them back into line? In Europe, the shift was made easy by never abandoning the necessary spokes. Urban railroads, just like urban roads, still radiated in all directions. Without comparable urban railroads, Amtrak was already making promises it could never keep.

Alone, Amtrak could never rebuild the connectivity now lost to suburban roads. In Europe, railroads encouraged and preserved those linkages, and intercity trains drew from many corridors, recharging them in return. Streetcars, subways, and light-rail systems had been part of suburban planning. In Europe, those systems had helped preserve the central city; in the United States, everything called a downtown was on the rocks.

Amtrak asked the impossible of suburbanites: forget the newer, superior connectivity of the highway; return instead to the past, because we promised Congress that you would. Ignore the comfort and convenience of the automobile for the dilapidated uncertainty of public transportation. If necessary, take a cab to the railroad station. Park your car in a crumbling neighborhood. Just get here so we can keep telling Congress you are the future of passenger rail.

It could not work, and did not work, at least not as Amtrak claimed. Even the best urban transit systems in the Northeast were but shadows of their European counterparts. Meanwhile, who had not heard of someone being attacked on public transit? Who had not seen buses and subway cars covered with graffiti, their stations becoming eyesores? Who would want to use those facilities to connect with Amtrak?

Nevertheless, in 1976 Amtrak promised Congress it would triple the number of intercity riders in the Northeast Corridor—by 1990[1]—but there was no way Amtrak could keep the promise. How were suburbanites, without their cars, to get back and forth between the trains? Where was the safe and clean public transportation needed between the suburbs and downtown? Where were the spokes, the variety of urban railroads, that Europe had and America lacked?

In the end, the Northeast Corridor was just a corridor—just a sliver across the landscape. Riders needed to be enticed to come back to it. The same went for everything in between. What led Congress to believe that people would get back in line for Amtrak when roads could take them everywhere?

Amtrak was lucky the Corridor had even stabilized, but the airlines did not relax their competition. By 1993, the Northeast Corridor was still in a rut, and averaged barely 11 million intercity passengers a year—not even half of the 30 million promised seventeen years before.[2] Obviously, the theory that a larger population meant more riders had egregious flaws. Just because the Northeast was building itself into a megalopolis did not mean Amtrak alone would be tapping into it, nor especially that Amtrak would enjoy a virtual monopoly simply because its stations were still downtown.

Beginning in 1983, Amtrak managed something of a monopoly in the Corridor by contracting to run commuter services. But these were existing patrons, true commuters, not new intercity passengers.[3] Meanwhile, the temptation remained to discount any success outside the Northeast Corridor as a statistical aberration. If five hundred people were riding a long-distance train, Congress could be assured it was a fluke. As Amtrak's vice president of marketing put it to me in 1977, "But Al, I don't want the cowboys-and-Indians market." And so he complained and then explained about the reason long-distance trains would eventually die: cites in the West were too far apart. He made no bones about it—tourism was not a legitimate reason for Amtrak to be in business.

Soon afterward, President Jimmy Carter's administration used virtually the same argument. In 1979 the Secretary of Transportation, Brock Adams, asked for Amtrak's head—cutting up to a dozen long-distance routes. Why do "you people in the rail groups," Congress probed during the hearings, persist in defending those "frivolous" trains? There again was the double standard. To be taken seriously, trains had to be carrying business travelers. Of course, no one was telling that to the airlines flying tourists to Disneyland and Las Vegas.

Government statistics had already proved the pleasure market as the greatest motivation for travel. For each person traveling on business, three travel for tourism (including visits to friends and relatives). For all long-distance carriers, the proportion still holds today.[4] Indeed, when collecting the revenue, no one seems to care why people travel. It was in defense of the Northeast Corridor—in defense of a bloated prediction—

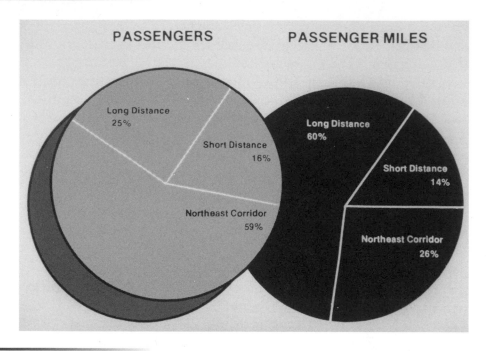

Data from Amtrak's 1976 Annual Report, contrasting number of passengers and passenger miles, proved an unexpected embarrassment to the company and bolstered critics' assertions that the long-distance trains outperformed the Northeast Corridor. Author's collection.

that Amtrak came to care. No pleasure travelers here, thank you, just people proving their seriousness by carrying a briefcase.

Amtrak headquarters itself, located in downtown Washington, encouraged tunnel vision. Just a block away at Union Station began the linear rat race. All Amtrak could see were the tracks it owned. It is no wonder the rail advocacy movement itself had begun to split, westerners now arguing that eastern activists ignored the needs of the entire country. No one in the West denied the importance of corridors; the West had several major ones of its own. Population density and a commitment to the business community would always be major draws. It was just that the West remembered better what trains had meant to the environment. The region's vision of itself remained one of stewardship, as reflected too in its railroads. Right up until the first day of Amtrak service, the West's trains overall had been the finest. Inevitably, that heritage motivated the West no less than feelings of an emerging megalopolis motivated the East. Both services were needed, and both eminently viable. It was only tunnel vision claiming otherwise.

Meanwhile, although Amtrak refused to admit it, the company owed its survival to the long-distance trains. What had saved the passenger train was the thrill of discovery, especially in the West. As reporters and writers clambered aboard the trains, they found a different Amtrak. They found Americans willing to more openly discuss the fact that highways and airports were heavily subsidized. No one, those passengers believed, need apologize for wanting trains. Although serving business markets remained important, seeing the country mattered as much or more.

The conviction was so strong that even Amtrak was forced into planning new equipment for its long-distance trains. Of course, Amtrak might continue to disparage the need (and did so) by following the lead of the railroads and asserting that most long-distance riders were selfish (again the word used was frivolous) to equate travel with enjoyment. As a point of legitimate travel, no fare paid to see the country could have the same importance as a fare paid for business travel in the Corridor.

It is in cases like these that history notes with amusement the proverbial right hand not knowing what the left is doing. Suddenly, Amtrak's 1976 annual report leaked the fiscal truth: nationwide, long-distance routes accounted for a whopping 60 percent of passenger miles. It followed that if Amtrak killed its long-distance markets, three-fifths of its revenue would be gone. In fiscal 1976, of the 18.2 million people who had traveled on Amtrak, 59 percent (nearly 11 million) had used the Northeast Corridor. Another 14 percent (roughly 2.5 million patrons) had traveled short-distance routes outside the Corridor. Combined, those 13.5 million people were an impressive number, but they had not gone far enough. The blow to Amtrak's ego was that it could not survive without the West and the South, where just 4.5 million riders were generating three-fifths of all Amtrak sales.[5]

Hoisted by its own petard, Amtrak tried using another argument: long-distance trains were just more expensive to run. (Of course, it was better not to mention the incentive program—a real drag on profitability.) Critics lamented, how could it be more obvious—Amtrak was meant to fail. Why else would the company disparage *any* source of revenue, and especially its major source? Why could Amtrak not just admit that no train made a profit. Cutting the long-distance trains would do nothing but force the costs of Amtrak onto fewer trains.[6]

Besides, the long-distance market was hardly insular. Passengers arriving in Boston, Washington, and New York on long-distance trains also made connections to the Corridor. Would they stick around if the long-distance trains got the ax? Historically, the long-distance markets themselves had not been maximized, including ski trains and seasonal excursions to the national parks. Why not have more of those, and ensure that all trains arrive at better hours? In season, why not a second train running opposite the existing schedule, especially a nighttime schedule? Amtrak continued to wring its hands, protesting the added losses. Yet for business travelers in the Northeast Corridor, it added that second train and many more.

It was hard not to conclude that Amtrak was doing the railroads' bidding. These were its landlords' arguments, not the arguments of reform. Were the Corridor itself to be honestly profitable, it needed ridership in the tens of millions. Even then, the government needed to pay the capital costs just as it did for any airline. Speed called for a new airport (superior tracks), not just modern trains with no place to land. Round-the-clock safety required intensive, costly maintenance. As early as 1976, estimates for a total upgrade of the Northeast Corridor ranged as high as $3.5 billion, more than triple Amtrak's annual budget. Clearly, it was an investment difficult to justify if those additional riders failed to appear.[7]

The obvious temptation (again denied) was to gamble everything on the Corridor. First Amtrak needed to get the genie back in the bottle. Subsequent annual reports dropped the comparison of long- and short-distance passenger miles. Only total miles were reported, and a new statistic emerged: passenger miles per train mile.[8] Both allowed Amtrak to float the argument that greater distances explained greater losses. Because the long-distance trains traveled farther and carried more passengers, they invariably cost more to run.

If this was true, it could only be because Amtrak was being overcharged and, indeed, ignoring history. In the railroads' view, what was Amtrak meant to accomplish but the death of the passenger train? As it stood, the railroads had always believed in mystifying the public as to how they arrived at profits and losses, a problem worsened by government regulation and the imposed accounting formulas.

By the 1960s, all of this meant that railroad accounting had been politicized. Indeed, "Hamlet's ghost," reported Stanley Berge in the *Journal of Marketing*, "could not have haunted the passenger train more than the ICC's ancient cost-separation formula dating from 1887, which has remained virtually unchanged since 1914." That formula, he elaborated, "requires the railroads each year to charge passenger trains with millions of dollars of costs, most of which could not be eliminated by removal of all passenger trains." The losses were not real, "but largely 'bookkeeping phantoms'." But so had the railroad industry, Berge charged, "done little to persuade the ICC to change its ancient ways."[9]

As professor of transportation in the business school at Northwestern University, Berge proved a serious critic. His ability to write for general audiences only added to his prestige. For a time, his articles and reports rocked the industry. Then, with the establishment of Amtrak, Berge's work was dismissed as history—but Berge had gotten too near the truth. Any side of a business can be made to look unprofitable when it is actually not. If a business wishes to maximize its profits elsewhere, that truth is not what management wants.

No valid economics need cloud Amtrak's preferences, either. It wanted the Northeast Corridor, the only tracks it would ever own. If in the 1970s Amtrak was picking favorite routes, consider again its cultural baggage. Without the clarity of a national purpose, everything about railroads was schizophrenic. The railroads were pulling in one direction, Amtrak in another, and Congress in yet another. In these narrowing agendas, what was deemed fiscal outrage was often nothing more than rhetoric from the opposing side. Railroads facing bankruptcy liked Amtrak well enough when their checks arrived. For some, Amtrak had suddenly become their biggest customer and, when it came to payment, their most reliable. The railroads could also see that a Northeast Corridor rebuilt by the government was another way of subsidizing them for moving freight. In the midst of conflicting claims and hidden agendas, there were few leaders separating fact from fiction. Why have passenger trains anywhere, the nation might reasonably ask, if the need for them could not be explained?

The nationwide passenger system survived the bickering only because of public confidence. Ultimately, Americans rejected the idea of saving the passenger train by pitting one part of the country against another. In the end, America knew the score: one kind of train was not inherently better than another, nor was Amtrak getting the only subsidy. Every mode of transportation was heavily subsidized, and singling out Amtrak did not change the truth.

Simply put, aesthetic and civic-minded concerns had overcome the drag of culture. Rather than believe Amtrak or the railroads, the public retreated to common sense. The typical American citizen ignored the experts, suspecting that Professor Berge was right: all the players had a hidden agenda. Perhaps the public did not understand the economics, but then, what economist really did?

The public, just wanting trains, was more than willing to pay for them. Like the national parks, those few trains still binding the continent seemed no less American, no less worthwhile. Trains of distance, overcoming lines and cities, just seemed good to have. It was not Amtrak's thinking, and most certainly not the railroads' thinking, but they were suffering from tunnel vision. The public, before opening its wallet, had long before opened its eyes.

chapter 9

Home Again,
and Santa Barbara

If the consequence of losing the passenger train was to lose the American landscape, consider how many people today cannot see the loss. For them, suburbia is reality. Nature begins farther and farther away, now only in wilderness areas or national parks. Increasingly, the idea of beauty as a living experience is from America's past. The progressive city demanded close-in nature. There should be sidewalks and tree-lined boulevards, generous flower beds, and urban parks. Today the boulevard is likely called an arterial. It is missing trees and sprouting billboards. And the city park—if there is a park—is more about soccer fields than urban nature.

In Binghamton, the progressives' vision had been obvious in the view of the Susquehanna River revealed across the rooftops of my neighborhood. Near the heart of the city, where the Chenango River joined the Susquehanna, there was a tree-lined park. I could walk or ride my bicycle into this natural corridor, my object not necessarily recreation, but to just enjoy the beauty of the riverbank. There the city, although always visible, could be out of mind. Meanwhile, whichever route I had chosen to the river, there was a worthy park along the way. Nothing approximated the dream of wilderness, but again, wilderness was not the point. It was rather that no citizen should have to search for beauty. The intention of the progressive city (and the progressive landscape) was always to respect nature in daily life.[1]

Unavoidably, the battle for wilderness in the twentieth century overtook the progressives' dream. The irony is that the movement never intended the fragmentation between landscape and wilderness; the greater goal was inclusiveness. Accommodating change was one thing, losing natural beauty quite another. The city and the countryside should be no less beautiful just because the nation needs separate wilderness areas.

As the key to civic pride, beauty was also a foundation of public health. Linking poverty and despair with ugliness, the progressives saw natural beauty as the antidote.[2] Only when their hopes for urban America stalled did preservationists fixate on the public lands. Even then, there remained that larger battlefield—America the Beautiful. Did private property not have an obligation to physical beauty no less than public lands?

This is hardly a common claim today. A widening gulf between citizenship and consumerism finally trumped the progressive spirit; equating beauty with lowered crime rates, for example, seemed far-fetched in an age of consumption. As well, poverty seemed better described as the result of laziness rather than the absence of urban parks.

The progressives, that is the preservationists, had nonetheless tried their best. For them, establishing a flower bed or dismantling a billboard remained as important as establishing a national park. Preservationists wanted America the Beautiful—and the City Beautiful—decades before wilderness as we define the term today overrode those daily interests.

That ideal of moderation, of blending nature into the city, has been the big loser these past fifty years. The same may be said of the countryside Americans knew before 1950. Born on a farm 10 miles south of Binghamton, my mother recalled when urban and rural America were virtually one. Losing nearby farmlands to suburban sprawl was unthinkable at the time. Consider the distances today between a city and its food supply: lettuce comes from California, tomatoes from Mexico, and meat from who knows where.

The term "farmer's market" recalls when all those products came into the city from close at hand. Every Saturday my grandparents made the trip (initially by horse and wagon). Grandfather sold meat, milk, and vegetables; grandmother sold her fruit and preserves. When the progressives advocated a national countryside, they included my grandparents' farm. What Europe still means by a national countryside is that prime agricultural lands such as these must be saved.

The belief that there is always more land to be had shows the power of America's pioneer hangover. By the Progressive Era (the early twentieth century), huge hinterlands had already been developed for the production

of wheat, beef, and pork. And finally, refrigerated transport made it possible to enjoy the products of the world.[3] But no city then was as vulnerable to outside forces or, as the progressives reasoned, as vulnerable to the loss of beauty as cities are now.

Only because Binghamton lost industry and population has much of its open space still survived. But it is a landscape increasingly devoid of farms, and thus without their pastoral benefits. Houses and trailers dot the fields of yesteryear, their residents still tied to the nearest supermarket. Increasingly, former farm-to-market roads are used by commuters. As the roads are widened, trees disappear. Across the country, with the loss of bucolic nature, what was left for the progressives to claim but distant wilderness?

The point remains that progressives had hoped for a *national* landscape. The entirety of the American experience should resist consumptive, destructive change. No city should resign itself to the loss of beauty, whether internally or on the outskirts.

The ideal of balance between beauty and commercialism drove preservationists to support the passenger train. However, not all railroad landscapes were aesthetically pleasing—an added indictment of industrial corridors was the number of signs and billboards. Just as highways are now, railroads then were an inviting target; because advertising wished to follow people, it had naturally followed the railroads. Thus J. Horace McFarland, as president of the American Civic Association, penned bitterly in 1908, "The sun sets behind Crystal Domino sugar, and going west, should one's eyes open in the early morning to view the famous Horseshoe Curve in the Pennsylvania Alleghenies, he will find the mountain scenery punctuated by Harvard beer and cheap clothing. His sense of outrage will not decrease when he learns that the great Pennsylvania Railroad abhors these signs, and does all in its power to prevent their indecent intrusion upon its enterprise."[4]

The New York Central, McFarland further confirmed, prohibited tasteless advertising in its terminals, a policy actually in force since 1888, according to railroad officials.[5] Reporting in 1898, general passenger assistant George H. Daniels confirmed that the railroad had refused "a

This inviting brochure cover (ca. 1930) by the California artist Maurice Logan suggests the beauties of the Santa Barbara coastline, including the city's historic mission. Author's collection.

number of very flattering offers, so far as money was concerned, from parties who wanted to introduce a systematic method of advertising in stations along our line and on the right-of-way." Daniels had "steadily urged that such a use of our buildings and right-of-way would detract from the comfort of our patrons very much more than any advantage we should gain from a revenue thus derived." The operating department had fully supported him. Although the department was not aware that the railroad's "positive instructions" had been infringed, its superintendent was surely pleased to have "taken the matter up, and advised our Maintenance of Way Department to destroy all advertisements found along the line of the road."[6]

Progressivism wanted corporations to act responsibly without being asked. That railroads would ban billboards—and ban them willingly—went to the heart of why preservationists supported the railroads. It remained for the automobile to breach the railroads' discipline and everywhere dash their conviction that travelers should not be importuned. By the 1960s, only a few cities were themselves banning billboards; Binghamton, unfortunately, was no longer among them.

I would not find such a city again until arriving in Santa Barbara to begin my Ph.D. To be sure, it helped that Santa Barbara's natural setting is monumental. Behind it crest the Santa Ynez Mountains; the entire city looks out over the Pacific Ocean. By preserving those views, both the city and county had found it easy to be progressive, and banned all billboards, as had the New York Central. The setting further inspired a height limit on buildings and the establishment of city parks galore, including a promenade fronting the beach and a botanical garden high in Mission Canyon. In addition, there are state parks and county parks up and down the coast, and the Santa Ynez Mountains are part of Los Padres National Forest, further protecting them from unwanted change.

And yet, few probably noticed that final subtlety straight from the progressives' textbook. A railroad still commanded the water, and a long-distance passenger train still called in daylight. Tourists had begun descending on Santa Barbara in the 1880s after the coming of the railroad. Then the pattern had been a familiar one in California and the West: brochures and advertisements published by the Southern Pacific Railroad had alerted travelers to the city's wondrous climate, adding views of its inviting beaches, elegant mission, and glorious mountain backdrop.[7]

This was the city I found when I arrived in 1971. California may have been overly committed to freeways, but not skeptical Santa Barbara—that would destroy downtown. On holiday weekends, the backup of impatient motorists heading home to Los Angeles was often 5 miles long, with everyone forced through a series of aging stoplights. Regardless, Santa Barbara refused to budge. Why should the city cut itself in two?

Rather, citizen awareness had only been raised by the infamous Santa Barbara oil spill. In January 1969, an estimated 3 million gallons of crude had soiled the city's beaches and community harbor. Afterward, Santa Barbara was even more insistent that it had every right to oppose development. Offshore drilling in the Santa Barbara Channel should stop. Moderate change was one thing; capitulating to the automobile was quite another.

Thus I found Santa Barbara's progressivism, and even more its consensus, still very much intact. Whether as liberals or conservatives, a majority of residents feared the loss of their natural setting. The drilling platforms now threatening the city's beaches had already ruined the view of the ocean. In reviewing the wisdom of further development, the government should have to consider the entire region, and should do nothing along the coast that would threaten its uniqueness.

The point is that Santa Barbara's historical ally, the Southern Pacific Railroad, remained in a position to assist that mandate. Upwards of 150,000 people annually still saw Santa Barbara from a train. Stone-stepping above the surf, surrounded by mountains, sea, and sky, the Coast Route refocused for passengers why Santa Barbara mistrusted change. Even if only a few of those passengers understood progressivism—and even if environmentalists had forgotten the history—it was obvious, just by looking out the window, that Santa Barbara cared. No one need mention that its coastline was perhaps the most beautiful in North America. Nor need anyone confirm for arriving passengers that Santa Barbara was perhaps America's most beautiful city.

To be sure, beauty was the key word. Obviously, Santa Barbara had refashioned wilderness into something designed and formal. In wanting that formality, Santa Barbara was no different from any city—the differences were in the wish to remain progressive. Santa Barbara planned deliberately for natural values long after most cities had given up the mandate. Perhaps it was because Santa Barbara had started late, rebuilding after a 1925 earthquake that had ripped apart the downtown area.

Following pages: J. Craig Thorpe, *Pacific Coast at Gaviota, California*, 2005. Pen and ink, 15 x 22 inches. Collection of Deborah and Louis Steplock. Used by permission of the artist.

PACIFIC COAST AT GAVIOTA, CALIFORNIA

Forced to play catch-up, the city had finally listened intently to Pearl Chase, a determined activist who perfectly guided the city's approach to rebuilding. A city with such a noble setting should itself be something special—the city should not resort to common architecture, but rather build upon a true sense of California. A traditional architecture was called for, reprising Spanish and Moorish styles. The adoption of height restrictions would further ensure a city built to human scale. The best views would be enhanced, and Santa Barbara would not forget open space. It was a message straight from the heart of the progressive movement: refuse expedience on every hand. Any submission to aesthetic blight was merely an opening wedge to perpetual ugliness.

From the train, the new Santa Barbara still announced grandeur and expectation. First came miles of imposing coastline from the north, still as isolated as it was spectacular. As at Azilum and Wyalusing Rocks, this was a beauty having nothing to do with wilderness. Santa Barbara, thinking progressively, had sought to stabilize the urban and rural landscape. The object was not preventing change, but rather guiding it with purpose.

Now opposing the search for oil, concerned residents had formed a new organization, Get Oil Out! or GOO!. Predictably, because it had originated in Santa Barbara its members included the wealthy, among them movie stars and industrialists. A few kept up appearances, driving the Volkswagen Beetles and vans identified with California's hippie culture. Those exceptions aside, the parking lot told a different story: often, the very people opposed to oil drilling in the Santa Barbara Channel owned large, gas-guzzling cars.

Inevitably, it was the beginning of an inconsistency that besieged Santa Barbara as surely as it would have a struggling Binghamton. Values began to clash. The breathtaking Gaviota coast served as a reminder of Santa Barbara's classic past. On a clear day, I reveled in tracing the shoreline all the way back to the university. From the bluffs, it was also a perfect spot for watching whales or hawks soaring on the thermals. Like Azilum and Wyalusing, Gaviota taught that accessible beauty is the key to America the Beautiful, preserving what exists close to home.

As with my favorite eastern haunts, the major compromise remained the railroad. Preservationists had early considered Gaviota a worthy addition to the state park system. Even the pier laid across the breakers did not seem distracting. Standing above the waves, I enjoyed watching them boil beneath my feet. Occasionally, a big wave would send everyone running, and the ranger would close the pier—visitors loved it. Diehard wilderness enthusiasts need only imagine when the waves would finally win.

I was just happy to be there, generally to clear my mind from the trials and tribulations of graduate school, reminding myself what those goals were all about. Writing about wilderness, I reveled in this sliver of it. Nothing that had compromised Gaviota had erased the feeling. A large railroad trestle linking the bluffs also seemed out of mind until, hearing a train, everyone on the beach looked up and waved. Less than a mile to the south, a tank farm was also visible. However, the tanks (appropriately painted green) were veiled by trees—it did not yet appear that the search for oil had turned excessive. Cattle from nearby ranches dotted the hillsides, but again, the few buildings were subdued. Acknowledging those many decades of development, the landscape remained appealing. Gaviota was still the ideal progressive landscape, asserting that change need not overwhelm it.

Then abruptly, in 1978, a large drilling platform appeared in the channel. More platforms were expected, in which case all that oil would need to be brought ashore. Preparing it for shipment to refineries called for a processing plant, and Gaviota was said to be the ideal site.

By then I had left Santa Barbara, reminiscent of my escape from Binghamton, but Santa Barbara was also home. Returning to Gaviota in 1987, my worst fears would be realized. The processing plant, resembling a large refinery, defied the voice of progressivism I had known. The railroad's voice had been subdued, and Gaviota finally looked developed. The processing plant represented development saturation, a far cry from either accommodating change or allowing none at all.

If that could happen near a city renowned for preservation, I wondered if any landscape could resist. What had become of Wyalusing Rocks and the panorama that overlooked Azilum? The plans of the U.S. Army Corps of Engineers had been defeated, but had that made a difference? I had heard the rumors before heading west. The Pennsylvania Department of Transportation was insisting that U.S. Highway 6 was no longer adequate for heavy trucks. Azilum and Wyalusing Rocks were dangerous bottlenecks (or so state engineers alleged). Now that trucks were larger and cars much faster, portions of each overlook might have to go. At Wyalusing, tractor trailers climbing the hill had slowed motorists to a crawl, and people not interested in the scenery were beginning to lose their patience. Only a passing lane accommodated by a deeper cut would allow cars and trucks to share the highway safely while maintaining speed. Pedestrians crossing the road to go to cabins and souvenir shops were also dangerous, and thus those buildings should be demolished.

Unable to attend the public hearings, I left the story there. Engineers gave no assurances for Azilum, either. As with Gaviota, the question of what created the need was lost in the argument that change was needed. Unlike the Lehigh Valley Railroad, the new highway was not offering occasional interruptions, followed by a blissful return to nature. And the argument alleging improved safety for motorists assumed there would be constant traffic.

It would have been best had I not returned but rather left the warmth of my memories alone. Curiosity is a powerful thing—when I did return, Brad was with me and shared both my curiosity and my anxiety.

As I pointed the car uphill, both of us held our breath. We could see it was a new cut—and a big one—but what had happened to the rocks? Then we exited the cut, glanced to our left, and heaved a sigh of relief—they were still there! But the buildings had been removed. One dilapidated frame (we thought a cabin) was all that suggested the former layout. Opposite, disposable diapers, bottles, and beer cans lined the pathway to the rocks, and plastic bags clung to the trees. The Switzerland of America, as the Lehigh Valley Railroad had proudly called it, now came with a larger parking lot.

Had we not known the history, we never would have believed that a railroad had loved this place. Under the "care" of the highway department, the overlook had been destroyed. Vandals had turned even the rocks into a common scribble pad, then tossed their empty cans of spray paint where we once lingered in the cool of the evening. We recalled the rocks in the days of the old road, encouraging nothing but awe and respect. Had our singing reached the river? Was the moonrise as beautiful down below? This was no place for graffiti rants and ravings. Why had the highway engineers not thought of that?

Railroad engineers had thought of it, just as highway engineers had learned not to care. Now all a highway needed to do to conquer a landscape was argue for a motorist's right to speed. It was no wonder the twists and turns of history were being vanquished everywhere. With the railroads no longer teaching stewardship, why would any highway respect that ideal?

Historically, the railroad's respect for landscape had prompted Pennsylvania to protect the rocks. Over the years, the Lehigh Valley Railroad sent poets, writers, and artists to this spot to promote the preservation of everything they could paint or describe. Now the greater landscape had lost its ally. Easing the grade for heavy trucks, Pennsylvania had abandoned stewardship. The freight in those trucks should have been on the railroad, and Wyalusing Rocks should still be teaching Pennsylvania to love the land.

There could be no question what awaited us at Azilum. Its ramshackle appearance heightened our sadness, and we turned the car for home. How was it possible, we asked? Two landscapes that had changed our lives now filled us with despair.

We recalled that railroads had been single-minded but not blinded by indifference. I remembered another perfect story. Robert Louis Stevenson, the future author of *Treasure Island,* had arrived by train in 1879 and immediately upon seeing the river at Harrisburg, asked a brakeman for its name. "Susquehanna," the brakeman had replied, filling Stevenson with delight. The resonance of its name struck the young Scottish author as "part and parcel of the beauty of the land." Susquehanna "was the name, as no other could be, for that shining river and desirable valley."[8]

It seemed best that Brad and I end our discussion there, like Stevenson, mindful that much of the Susquehanna River was still shining and one day, reclaimed by railroads, might even inspire the restoration of Wyalusing Rocks.

chapter 10

Gateway to Wilderness

In late August 1977, I resolved to see Glacier National Park. I wished to prove, if only to myself, that somewhere the progressives' dream of American travel still instructed and inspired.

Indeed, the lingering magic of my trip was a chance to experience the history. The slogan "See America First" headlined the Progressive Era. The establishment of Glacier National Park in 1910 had been all about turning wealthy easterners away from Europe. The Great Northern Railway had called them west with patriotism—see America first. In establishing Glacier, Congress awarded the railroad a national park right on its doorstep. From the park, a main line went all the way to Chicago, and from there to every city in the East. No other railroad had a main-line

It is April 1916 and the Great Northern Railway is advertising its newest hotel in Glacier National Park, Many Glacier, on Lake McDermott (now Swiftcurrent Lake). Note the visitor count from 1915—"twenty thousand strong." Obviously, the Great Northern Railway found something in that figure to cheer about, possibly that long-distance passengers were very lucrative. Author's collection.

park. No wonder the Great Northern had been inspired; this could be a true Switzerland of America. Besides, that other Switzerland required a steamship. To reach Glacier, the patriotic tourist just needed to step on the train.

By 1977, that history had all but disappeared. Yellowstone, Yosemite, and the Grand Canyon had already lost their passenger trains. Many tracks serving the national parks were gone or soon to be abandoned, and with abandonment would come the salvage crews. Mount McKinley still welcomed passenger trains, but all connections were inside Alaska. Only Glacier connected with the continent, and wondrously, all of it by rail. No car or airplane was required. Obviously, this last outpost of progressive travel owed its survival to a stroke of luck. As a major transcontinental railroad, the route to Glacier was deemed essential for national commerce.

Intellectually, it was a journey I had made in 1974, when, in a series of articles for *National Parks and Conservation Magazine*, I had called for restoring history's "pragmatic alliance" between preservationists and the railroads.[1] Especially during an energy crisis, this alliance might serve to keep the parks secure. But this was my first visit to Glacier and, fortunately, its train survived. Still, if I wanted to experience some firsthand history, it seemed advisable to get cracking. Soon that train might vanish too. By 1977, Arab oil was flowing again; Prudhoe Bay in Alaska was coming on line. Undoubtedly, America would forget the energy crisis and get right back into cars.

In any case, I intended to play the part thoroughly. How light could I possibly travel—how had Americans packed for wilderness in the days of rail? Historical photographs told me I was probably giving the past too much credit here—Americans have always packed too much. Fortunately, I need not take a tent or sleeping bag, since the progressives had believed in hotels. I would stay in the lodge at East Glacier. That was progressivism, I rationalized, knowing that environmentalism would not be convinced. It was the age of backpacking, after all. An environmentalist purity of motive demanded that in entering wilderness, one should reject civilization outright. Progressivism had not been so intolerant. Besides, I still planned hiking as much as possible, for which I took the basics: boots, canteen, and jeans.

Further striving for historical legitimacy, I used public transportation the entire way. Still a resident of Santa Barbara, I departed by bus from my apartment. Downtown, I could either walk or transfer to the railroad station, about ten blocks from the transit center.

As usual, the bus was cramped with little space to stow my gear. Here is the first problem, I thought to myself. A city bus in the United States discourages a broader connectivity with intercity transportation. The supposition is that everyone is commuting. I consoled myself with the knowledge that the train would have lots of space for storage. Meanwhile, I chalked up a point for automobiles. Ignoring the privacy argument, it was a matter of convenience: throw your stuff in the trunk and be on your way.

Rather than transfer to another bus, I walked the half mile to the depot. Once again, the *Coast Starlight* was running late; with Labor Day around the corner, it was also jammed. Fortunately, half the passengers were getting off in Oakland, which promised to free extra seats. I hoped to spread out for the night without someone nodding off at my elbow.

Obviously, even my mind-set was still thinking car—still thinking privacy. A train functions on the conviction that there are some things a car can never do. In my case, I needed only to see the ocean. By that time I had lost count how often I had participated in this ritual. Magically, that first sighting of the water seemed to soothe everyone on the train; something about the waves was always different. Best of all, with the railroad claiming the ocean side of the bluffs, the view was unobstructed.

These were the miles I had intended to relish over lunch in the dining car. I dumped my luggage and headed there—securing my seat could wait till later. Since a large load always boarded at Santa Barbara, the conductors might take an hour to collect the tickets, and by then the dining car would have filled and I would lose a table facing the surf. It appeared I already was too late, so I took a five-dollar bill from my wallet and agreed to wait for my favorite side. "No need to wait, sir," the steward replied, accepting the money with a smile. "A couple of folks are leaving shortly; I'll have a place cleaned for you in a jiffy."

Five minutes later he seated me opposite a couple from New York. "Have you ever seen anything more beautiful?" the woman asked her husband, glancing briefly in my direction. "What do you mean by 'beautiful'," he replied, "the ocean or those people down there mooning us?" In the aisle seat and not next to the window, she could not see below the tracks to the beach and so had missed the entire show. "We call them nudie beaches," I announced, insisting they were common. "The surfers do have their sense of humor."

She laughed and the ice was broken. The train was taking over. Our first shared experience dropping behind us (literally and figuratively), we talked away the miles. They were getting off in Oakland and would return east via Denver and Chicago. It was a great route, I assured them. They should look for the American River Canyon as they climbed the west face of the Sierra. After the summit they should watch for Donner Lake and the Truckee River Canyon. For me? A new route, too, I answered, the *Starlight* to Seattle and the *Empire Builder* across to Glacier National Park.

During the tourist season, the Great Northern Railway added open-air observation cars along the boundary of Glacier National Park and on trains crossing Stevens Pass in Washington State. Dome cars replaced open-air observation in the late 1940s and 1950s. Original Great Northern Railway photograph, ca. 1920. Author's collection.

They had done that last year, they confided, smiling widely with enthusiasm. I would absolutely love it.

Under the circumstances, I could hardly complain about having to share a seat north of Oakland. Typically, the train was merely exchanging one load of passengers for another, so I decided to meet some of the new arrivals. The best people-watching was always in the lounge. Besides, I wanted to confirm a rumor—that the lounge car this leg of the trip would smell heavily of marijuana.

Smell it did, and then some. In his 1975 novel, *Ecotopia,* Ernest Callenbach had identified this part of the West Coast as a stronghold of America's counterculture.[2] In the rugged outback north of San Francisco, growing marijuana was the norm and the patches were easy to hide. Obviously, the growers had also discovered this train, plying it back and forth to the Bay Area, which was their biggest market. They were now talking freely: the feds could not possibly patrol every national forest, they said. It was best to pick a rugged spot, well up a hillside, where the "fat rangers" would never go. Ecotopia was indeed full of hard-to-get places where few rangers had ever tread.

I could hardly believe my ears. Were these people not afraid of being arrested? Apparently not, because suddenly plastic bags were popping open, their contents spilling onto blemished paper. The whole lounge car was filling with smoke. It was true—the *Coast Starlight* was the Marijuana Express. I just had to sit there to get high. Obviously, William Jefferson Clinton never rode the *Starlight* because, trust me, he would have inhaled.

Seriously, where were the conductors? I asked myself. But again, I already knew the answer. All the conductors worked for the Southern Pacific Railroad—they had no worries about getting paid, no matter how many passengers might keel over. Besides, the other passengers had retreated; the car was all pot-smokers now. Any complaints would go to Amtrak, not the Southern Pacific, which could point out that Amtrak owned the train.

Fortunately, my companion up in coach neither snored nor smelled of marijuana, so I did get a good night's sleep. It was all new to me in the morning—we followed a spectacular forested path across the spine of the Cascade Range, and then dropped and dropped, twisting and turning out of the heights into Oregon's fabled Willamette Valley. The pioneers of the Oregon Trail had considered this valley a good reason to brave five months of pain and hardship.

The train split the center of the valley, following both history and farming as it headed north. The Cascade Range was now to our right, and upon reaching Portland, we could see Mount Hood guarding the Columbia River, splendidly framed by the city's skyline. Crossing the river into Washington State, Mount Saint Helens briefly displayed its summit. All that beautiful symmetry was volcanic, yet hinted nothing of plans to blow itself apart three years hence. Next in line came the largest dormant volcano, Mount Rainier, but its cloud cover disappointed us, obscuring all but the foothills. Perhaps this was Mother Nature's way of insisting we had had enough grandeur for one day. No matter, my connection with the *Empire Builder* required a layover in Seattle. From King Street Station, I called the Roosevelt Hotel, which was offering a special

Released in 2000 as a poster and menu cover, this painting found even Amtrak willing to celebrate the historic relationship between the *Empire Builder* and Glacier National Park. The train in the painting is eastbound, arriving at East Glacier Park station, with all of Glacier's wondrous heritage (including a jammer) looking on. J. Craig Thorpe, *Wilderness Threshold*, 2000. Oil on canvas, 18 x 24 inches. Used by permission of the artist.

rate for railroad passengers. By all means, the clerk agreed, she would give me a window facing Mount Rainier. I hoped the weather would cooperate, unveiling the summit in the morning.

I took a cab, also at a reduced rate, part of the hotel's package. Obviously, the Roosevelt was being creative, tapping into Amtrak customers in need of making this connection. The absurdity of it all filled my notes: How was Amtrak to compete for the pleasure traveler by making the schedule inconvenient at every opportunity? How many people would go out of their way to pay the extras—the added meals and a room in a hotel just for the privilege of taking trains? How many passengers was Amtrak losing just by failing to guarantee same-day connections with its most popular routes? Amtrak's scheduling decisions flew in the face of common sense, with difficult connections and so many single trains, many not even daily.

A clearing sky the following morning lifted my mood with the clouds. Mount Rainier was out! I thanked the rain gods and hailed a cab for King Street Station. On arrival, the waiting *Empire Builder* further pronounced that my inconvenience had been worth it—the train sported a full-length dome car, *Prairie View*. Best of all, the car had been spotlessly cleaned. A second dome in the rooftop of my coach offered the original configuration—half as many seats as the great dome but superior visibility forward. Even the Progressive Era had not seen trains as grand as this. Domes were added in the 1950s, the heyday of air-conditioned observation. We departed on time, five minutes before noon, the sun now beaming off the ice fields of Mount Rainier.

Naturally, I had perched myself in *Prairie View*. I decided against taking notes; the scenery was too incredible for that distraction. We headed south, then turned east at Auburn. Intervening ridges now blocked Mount Rainier as we began our ascent toward Stampede Pass, where its historic 2-mile tunnel awaited us. Rainier's summit briefly loomed above the trees, then we plunged into the darkness. Just as I had adjusted to the gloom, we exploded into light on the other side, descending through another forest flanked by mountains on both sides.

The conversation in *Prairie View* remained respectfully muted, punctuated occasionally by oohs and ahs. I had already exchanged introductions with a doctor and his wife who were escorting their daughter to college. They had described leaving their home in Peoria, Illinois, and boarding a train for San Francisco. Their daughter would attend Washington State University, so they had come north on the *Starlight* ahead of me and were getting off the *Empire Builder* in Spokane. There they would rent a car, drive to Pullman, and, after settling their daughter in, return to the *Empire Builder* three days later. It was also my schedule, I was pleased to note. Following my three days in Glacier, I would be continuing east to see my mother in New York.

I reflected again how observation on a train, especially these dome cars, had worked historically for the national parks. Granted, the ability of a train to mold consensus may have been unintended and unforeseen, but it was still that untangling of individualism that had meant so much to preservation. With the automobile, it was open season on lands adjacent to the roads—a pulling off here, a pulling off there, until everything became pockmarked with development. A highway is competition—even the same goal becomes a competition, everyone is intent on arriving. Aboard the *Empire Builder* we were equals and, most important, preservationists. We were also fast becoming friends; we were sharing the landscape, not simply viewing it, and the landscape was shaping us.

Next, the cliffs of the Yakima River Canyon towered above *Prairie View*, visible from the river to the skyline. Exiting the canyon, Mount Adams loomed in the distance. Why would any of us want to leave this car? Perhaps for lunch, my new friends suggested, as it was last call in the dining car. But yes, we should hurry back—which we did, to laze away the rest of the afternoon. I took pictures, catching the good doctor beaming. "I love this," he said, adding, "Life's great at sixty-two!"

At dinner, we asked the steward the name of the darkening river now on our right. "The Snake," he replied. "By the way, nice to have you back." Spokane would be getting close. We resisted our good-byes, promising to meet a final time on the platform. I wished Elizabeth good luck in school, aware that such farewells are generally permanent. "Don't get eaten by a bear, Professor Runte," she replied, grinning mischievously from ear to ear. "My folks are looking forward to having you along the rest of the way."

Then they passed through the station and disappeared. I noted, in consolation, that the train had done its job splendidly. As drivers we would have been isolationists. In an airplane we might have talked, although rarely as seriously or as deeply. Time would not have been on our side. One cannot feel a sense of loss until there has been a sense of sharing. Now, even if we never met again, this experience was ours for life. Such was the permanence of beauty and community that progressivism had always had in mind. Yet far distant, Glacier National Park was also the beneficiary. Our lesson would continue, with the *Empire Builder* teaching us to be better visitors. In the park, as we had aboard the train, we would welcome a chance to behave like preservationists.

I was finally thinking of my goal and as a first-time traveler, regretting only that all of Glacier National Park would be traversed in darkness. Good grief—why would anyone want to run these beautiful dome cars through a national park in the dead of night? The railroad paralleled Glacier's entire southern boundary; in daylight it was a breathtaking experience of nearly 60 miles. We would rendezvous with the park at 5:00 AM. The summer solstice two months behind us, that meant a sunrise arrival at East Glacier Park, effectively causing the passengers to miss every mountain, canyon, forest, and stream along the way.

How dumb, I thought, and what a comedown from the days of the Great Northern Railway. Then the railroad had virtually built the park, underwriting its chalets, major hotels, and miles of roads and trails. Every advertisement, calendar, guidebook, and poster had promoted Glacier mightily. The railroad commissioned three hundred paintings by the artist John Fery; Winold Reiss and Arnold Heinze had added hundreds more.

Many of the original paintings were hung where the public could see them—in ticket offices, waiting rooms, offices, and hotel lobbies. Nationwide, the railroad distributed reprints by the tens of thousands, emblazoned with the headline "See America First." The moment Glacier was established, the headline had been properly amended: "See America First via Glacier National Park." Normally, a second train—if not always the *Empire Builder* (or its predecessor, the *Oriental Limited*)—had ensured daylight scheduling for Glacier visitors. In 1977 the *Empire Builder* was the only train serving the route. But traveling through the heart of the Rocky Mountains in the middle of the night? Deadening darkness the *entire* way? Could there be any better proof that the bureaucrats at Amtrak headquarters had no clue about marketing trains?

That was a battle for another day, I decided. The train I was on was the one that mattered, and a beautiful train it had been—sparkling clean, on time, and staffed by a gracious crew. There had been other spectacular scenery to compensate for the scenery we would miss. I reminded myself that progressive thinking still asked for that larger goal: the whole of landscape, not just the national parks, merited our reverence and respect.

Snatching catnaps during the night, I watched our progress from the forward dome. Finally, the train's headlight had begun illumining tunnel portals and veering cliffs. Soon we were following a river off to our left, its rapids caught in the probing light. I squinted at my map, determining the river to be the Middle Fork of the Flathead. We are here, my watch was also telling me. This has to be Glacier National Park!

On we went, the laboring of the engines and the squeaking of the wheels informing me of mountains. Finally, it was nearing sunrise. A first hint of gray teased out a silhouette of mountains piling to our left, and in the slowly emerging colors, I could detect that the mountains ran parallel with the tracks. East Glacier should be behind those peaks. I left the dome, found my seat, and gathered up my belongings. The chair attendant was gliding through, quietly waking those who would disembark. "Ten minutes to East Glacier," he whispered. "May I take your luggage forward?" I assured him I could manage and hurried to peer out of the vestibule.

One of the Dutch doors was already open, spilling in the mountain air. A lake flashed by, then another, mirroring the streaks of warming light. What had been the blackened spears of evergreens now revealed their color against the dawn. Then we were slowing and rounding a bend, with rolling hills off to our right.

On our left, mountains still filled the horizon. "This is it," our attendant whispered. It seemed he was coaxing the train to fall silent so as not to disturb the sleeping passengers. Then he opened the door and locked the steps. "This is what you came for, sir," he said, helping me down with one hand and with the other gesturing toward the peaks. "Enjoy your stay." As he let go of my arm, I noticed that the tops of the mountains, which moments ago had been deep purple, were now splashed with a crown of rose. Everything to the east was glowing yellow. So here I was— on progressivism's doorstep. I had finally made it. This was the threshold of history and the threshold of stewardship that best reminded America what it had given up.

Suddenly the sunlight burst upon us, flooding past the station to the lodge. Every log and shingle clarified, the building seemed to rise and greet the mountains. Behind me, the *Empire Builder* was signaling good-bye, whistling its return to civilization. I waved briefly at the departing train, but without my normal regrets. Look at that lodge, I told myself. It is the *Empire Builder* standing still. It is all about the mountains too.

From the station, a pathway profusely lined with flower beds led up to the entrance. Another progressive touch, I delighted, confirming that beauty is both tame and wild. Okay, the teepee was a bit corny, but I recognized that it came with a long history. The Great Northern Railway had hired the Blackfeet to greet the trains of yesteryear, but that could be debated either way. For now, I watched the other passengers on the pathway and saw them top the rise. Their rubbernecking said it all. Who would not marvel that such a place—and such a train—had managed to survive all these years? I reached down for my luggage and followed them home.

Designing for Nature

The conviction that the national parks are overcrowded ignores the fact that numbers alone are not the problem. A proper design for each park is the challenge. The Glacier Park lodge greeting my arrival had been designed with its surroundings in mind. People might use it and not overwhelm those surroundings. It remained the perfect emblem of progessive thinking. Whether protecting wilderness, the city, or rural America, harmony was the key word.

Finally, environmentalists had dared suggest that harmony was impossible; it was time for absolutes. "No more cars in the national parks," demanded the wilderness curmudgeon Edward Abbey. "Let the people walk. Or ride horses, bicycles, mules, wild pigs—anything—but keep the automobiles and the motorcycles and all their motorized relatives out."[1] Abbey's tirade substantiated another common charge: environmentalists despised all use of wilderness but their own.

Even though Abbey had discovered the Utah wilderness as a ranger at Arches National Monument, he confessed in his book *Desert Solitaire* that outside of wilderness he loved the car. Off duty, he loved driving his pickup fast. "Over the rocky wagon road—that trail of dust and sand and washouts which I love, which the tourists hate so deeply—I go jouncing, banging, clattering in the old Chevvy [*sic*], scaring the daylights out of the lizards and beetles trying to cross the road. Stepping harder on the gas I

speed over the sand flats at 65 mph, trailing a funnel of dust about a mile and a half long."[2]

Although *Desert Solitaire* had proved a hit with environmentalists, history remained more skeptical. Cynicism aside, what was Abbey's solution for protecting parks and wilderness? The national parks needed a practical aesthetic allowing the survival of visitors. As a political construct, all wilderness required was that the government approve its boundaries. Logically, if environmentalism belittled the American experience, few Americans would go along. There had to be a better way of protecting wilderness than labeling civilization as its greatest threat.

At Glacier, my shining introduction to an earlier solution was the *Empire Builder* and this hotel. Now, even my environmental friends were flying into Kalispell or Missoula, bragging they had saved two days over traveling by train. In the next breath, they opposed drilling for oil in Alaska or off the Pacific Coast. How could they not see the connection? Without building responsibility into their actions, how could wilderness survive? The *Empire Builder* stood for accountability with distance as the instigator. Rather than insulting the public at the gate of wilderness, even jesting that they should ride pigs and mules, accountability meant asking the public to protect wilderness by accepting the necessary restraints—like trains.

Why should arriving at wilderness be all about saving time, at the cost of losing the American landscape? By their very nature, trains asked that question. Whether traveling near or far, no one should rush the land. To travel cross-country in the early days of the *Empire Builder* was to build stewardship into the trip. I estimated how many cars would still be needed to replace this single train. Without it, in 1977 its 25,000 Glacier-bound passengers would have needed 15,000 cars. In the normal three-month season, the train was displacing an average of 166 cars per day, still more than enough to be noticed on the park's narrow, twisting roads.

To be sure, it was the automobile that had changed the parks. Motorists sold on the idea of individualism had grown resentful of twists and turns. Further pressured by concessionaires, the Park Service

Beginning in the 1910s, motor stages (later nicknamed "jammers") were introduced to the national parks as appropriate for scenery and community travel. This ad appeared in 1916. We can see through the stage to the mountains and lake beyond, reassuring us that preservation is the vehicle's priority. Author's collection.

had generally played along. Over time, the design of a road was less about fitting visitors to the parks and more about accommodating the increasing size of motor vehicles. Again, invention drove legitimacy. If Detroit could make a bigger car and call it a sport utility vehicle, invariably the parks must accommodate its use.

The classic lament of the process is captured in Aldo Leopold's statement, "It is the expansion of transport without a corresponding growth of perception that threatens us with qualitative bankruptcy of the recreational process. Recreational development is a job not of building roads into lovely country, but of building receptivity into the still unlovely human mind."[3] With few exceptions, the unlovely side of the American mind had now slipped behind the wheel, reassured that however the car affected the environment, its existence as an invention still made it right.

If Glacier had proved resistant to unwanted change, it was because the *Empire Builder* had survived. A technology teaching reasonableness had survived. The subtlety was hidden until you thought about it, as I was doing now, noting that one of Glacier's bright red "jammers" had pulled up to the lodge. Like the *Empire Builder,* the jammer was another survivor from the age of reason. It was a bus, but hardly one of those behemoths that smack of corporate tourism. Rather, it was a bus designed to act like a train, extending the ethics of stewardship throughout the park. The models still used in Glacier during the 1970s were survivors from the 1930s. Even the nickname had to be explained now—jammers referred to jamming gears, since they originally came with standard shifts.

Otherwise, nothing about a jammer's intimacy or aesthetic beauty equated with corporate busing. Above all, the jammer imparted an art of scale, a careful crafting to time and place. There were bench seats instead of seats off an aisle, every seat accessible through a separate door; there was just a single step. In contrast, corporate buses were all about waiting to board through a single door and climbing steps. The constant sight of passengers lining up to wait their turn confirms the inconvenience and lack of intimacy.

Like all buildings, Glacier Park Lodge has evolved, including its magnificent lobby, shown here ca. 1920 when a form of western hodgepodge was in vogue. The great log pillars are Douglas fir with the bark on. Photo by T. J. Hileman, courtesy of the National Archives (photo 79-G-29A-5).

College students board buses at Gardiner Gateway to begin seasonal jobs in Yellowstone. The line of buses continues back into town. Imagine the traffic jam if buses carrying seventeen passengers were exchanged for cars holding three or four. Original Northern Pacific photograph, ca. 1940. Author's collection.

Critically, jammers were half or even a third the size of modern buses. Although the park roads of the 1920s and 1930s had demanded this size, in Glacier, it had come to be seen as planning—a park should plan for proper access, and roads should protect the scenery rather than pander to every vehicle. Larger vehicles, once appeased, would always demand appeasement. It is the American way to fatten everything and insist that bigger is better.

The jammers protected scenery and even attracted passengers from their cars with an intimacy few buses could hope to emulate. When necessary, a canvas covering placed along the roof supports protected the seats from rain and wind. However, the moment sunshine reappeared, the cover could as quickly be rolled back. I would later compare the sensation to the

Empire Builder, as if I were looking up through *Prairie View* without the glass. Although a convertible offered the same sensation, no driver should dare enjoy it.

Simply, a jammer invited respect for what the park was meant to be. The moment other parks had appeased tourism by scaling up their roads and parking lots, consumerism came rushing in. In Glacier, consumerism was still at bay. Here the jammer, like the *Empire Builder*, enlisted the visitor in preservation. More than a few cars were displaced. Just as important, those not displaced had the jammers as history's pace cars, reminding their occupants to appreciate the slower speed.

My walk between the railroad station and hotel entrance had been a revealing 150 yards, but I was not prepared for the time warp that greeted me when I crossed the threshold. Entering, I felt instantly moved to silence, as if I had come to stand in a great cathedral. It was a wooden structure and not one of limestone or precious marble. Still, the wood had the look of greatness. Massive trees, as standing pillars, supported a double tier of full-length balconies. A pitched roof opened to a skylight, allowing the sun's brilliance to flood throughout. "You'll get used to it," I heard a voice. The face to the voice was smiling. "May I check you in?" she asked. I closed my jaw and approached the counter, asking how she could be sure. She could still see my neck craning upward. "You will," she repeated confidently, "but it never does get tiring. This is my third summer working for the company, and this building never ceases to amaze me."

She had given me a room on the second floor, facing the station and not the mountains. It didn't matter, I had grown up with the sound of trains and would not be in the room until well after dark. Older people, unable to hike, should be given the mountain views. My first impression was the room's compactness—and no television. I further accepted the rustic simplicity as the encouragement of park values. Visitors were not supposed to be watching television, displacing those who wanted to see the park.

I vowed that another progressive, the novelist Mary Roberts Rinehart, should inspire my thinking here. Visiting Glacier in 1915, she had agreed that the accommodations met the test of appropriateness. "The great hotels are dwarfed by the mountains around them, lost in the trees," she reported. "Their domain extends no farther than their walls. The wilderness is there, so close that the timid wildlife creeps to their very doors."[4]

It was just what any progressive would have said. A sense of wilderness was not lost by building tastefully. Now that fifty-two years had passed, I wondered if my hotel still passed the test. After breakfast, I decided to find out. The clerk who had checked me in had mentioned a couple of trails behind the employee dorms; one branched off the service road, then headed up into the foothills. It was just the hike I was looking for, something accessible and close-in. If Rinehart was right, a short hike should easily prove her reasoning that park development need not intrude on wilderness.

After breakfast, I donned my hiking boots and retraced my steps through the lobby, still marveling at the rustic architecture. I had begun to notice something else—the attractive seating and the number of people just sitting around talking. Out the door I turned left, found the service road, and started walking toward the mountains. What if a bear attacked me here, I thought. That would certainly prove Rinehart's thesis, if not the part about timid wildlife!

Actually, bears in Glacier were no laughing matter. Just ten years earlier, in separate incidents, two women had been mauled and killed by grizzlies.[5] Wilderness means taking chances. John Muir repeatedly pointed out the chances we take in civilization—and Muir had died in 1914, before the automobile had seriously gotten started on its toll of deaths and injuries.

The greater danger lies in getting to the parks. Once there, visitors step off cliffs and drown in rapids, and yes, occasionally (although very rarely) some wild animal attacks and kills.[6] But, the car still beats them all. Three years later, as a seasonal ranger in Yosemite, I reminded visitors that automobile accidents by far outnumbered incidents caused by bears. Now, looking for the trail, my thoughts remained with Muir. Undoubtedly, this hike was about the safest thing I could do.

Enough, I finally decided, the morning is too beautiful for weighty matters. Ambling along the road, I finally found what appeared to be a path—it was either that or a winding cattle lane. I traced it carefully with my eyes, finally losing it high in a grove of aspens. A tinge of yellow already suggested fall. It looked scenically promising, so I turned off and started up. In minutes I had cleared the tree tops and was looking back across the plains. I could see what Rinehart had meant—I could barely make out the hotel, even though it was just a mile away.

Just a mile to be in wilderness, and I was not yet even officially inside the park. I wondered how much greater that distance might have been without the historical commitment to public transportation. In other

This Northern Pacific Railway brochure from 1913 confirms that park hotels were meant to rise from an unblemished landscape. In later years, the automobile and the demand for parking lots erased that sensation at Old Faithful Inn. Author's collection.

1913

THE LAND OF GEYSERS

•YELLOWSTONE • PARK•

large parks, especially Yellowstone, the same distance was becoming mean-ingless. There the Park Service, planning the centennial (1872–1972), had half surrounded Old Faithful in a sea of asphalt. Certainly, no overlook facing the Upper Geyser Basin recreated a feeling of what it had meant to be the first to stand there.

What if Glacier had as readily succumbed to the popularity of the car? What if Glacier, like Yellowstone, had lost its trains and jammers? What if nothing public-minded (or public-spirited) had instructed visitors on the qualities parks ought to achieve with development? Development might have ruined Glacier too, just as it seemed to be ruining Yellowstone.

Climbing higher, I tested the thesis from other vantage points, still grateful that every animal track pointed to cattle instead of grizzlies. Here I stood in the Rocky Mountains, and at no point since leaving Santa Barbara had I depended on a car. Why could that not have remained an option for every national park?

This was the proper feeling of parks—deeply wistful and ecstatic. It was more than just the problem of parks doubling and tripling visitation that deprived individuals of those feelings elsewhere. It was a problem of killing the teachers and then wondering why the pupils no longer learned. Just as Glacier's teachers had survived, Yellowstone's had been silenced. In the 1920s, there had been five railroads serving Yellowstone, at least one from each direction; two (the Northern Pacific and Union Pacific) offered branch lines to the boundary proper.

Finally Yellowstone lost them all, even its most distant connections, the trains arriving from Lander, Cody, Gallatin Gateway, and Red Lodge. The few jammers surviving in Yellowstone had no more trains to meet. Instruction in stewardship had been forgotten.

In Yellowstone, the loss of the trains and jammers led to dismantling the historical compromise. What had once been known as "parkitecture" (with timid wildlife creeping to the doors) has become surrounded with development. The celebrated Old Faithful Inn is now perched above a parking lot (a lighted lot, no less). At night, guard lights compete with the moonlight and starlight playing off the geysers. The lodge is out of context, no longer dwarfed by a natural and majestic foreground. A true progressive would have been appalled.

Even winter proved no deterrent. The air of benediction settling over Glacier's high country was on the run in Yellowstone. A recent decision to allow a limited number of snowmobiles in that park's Upper Geyser Basin had encouraged demands for even more of them.

In Glacier, the wonder of the seasons remained. On my mountain, nature still set the schedule, including its winter solitude. Already, fall's benediction was tangible in the slanting sunlight. A telling chill hung in the aspens. Most visitors would soon be leaving, giving the park back to the wildlife.

In Glacier, fall remained a benediction, instead of the beginning of another "shoulder season" (Labor Day through October). By selfishly lengthening the season, tourism has come to override preservation. For decades, the railroad, although bringing more tourists, had done nothing to disrupt seasonal closure. The last train out was exactly that. Leaving meant knowing it was time to go, believing that the park and its wildlife also needed a break from us. By the time I had scrambled back down the mountainside, the necessity of that break was clear. Although every ending is filled with sadness, this is how the national parks in September are supposed to feel.

As my first stop back at the hotel, I checked at the desk to read the forecast. Great! More sunshine for tomorrow, continuing brisk and clear. Perfect weather for riding the jammers, just as I had planned. I had an early dinner and went to bed. Having been awake much of the previous evening in the dome car, I suddenly felt the excitement catching up with me. Better to be rested than fatigued. My tour aboard the jammers would last all day.

In the morning I realized I had slept soundly and had not heard a passing freight. After breakfast I found my jammer, driven by a young man from Illinois. As soon as we boarded, he got right into his spiel. "Don't worry, folks," he announced. "I know all of these roads by heart attack. The last passenger who had one, by the way, agreed it was not my fault."

It was the beginning of a day of terrible jokes. The worst ended (we hardly needed the punch line) with a priest, a rabbi, a minister, and the driver of a jammer meeting Saint Peter at the pearly gates. Before they pass into Heaven, Saint Peter demands that all of them visit hell. Eternity is a long time, he reminded them. They might miss sex, develop a craving for booze, or discover they love rock and roll. Before he can allow them in, every sin tempting them must be resolved. But there is one exception: the driver was welcomed into heaven immediately. The other three are incredulous. "We have been ordained," they protest. "My point exactly," Saint Peter replies. "You have only sermonized against temptation. This young

Following pages: J. Craig Thorpe, *East of Glacier National Park, Montana*, 2005. Pen and ink, 15 x 22 inches. Collection of Deborah and Louis Steplock. Used by permission of the artist.

EAST OF GLACIER NATIONAL PARK, MONTANA

man drove jammers in Glacier National Park. Just thinking about it would be enough to scare the hell out of me!"

Although the commentary was simplified (why do tour guides always insist on being cute?), the experience of community was unmistakable. This was just a smaller train. Barely halfway through the day, we were talking like best friends. Together, we booed the driver's jokes, shared our film and cameras, and promised to send one another pictures. On the jammers, the same sense of community found on the *Empire Builder* flowed no less elegantly and equally by design.

The reach of that community was also unmistakable. People waved from cars, beside the road, at the turnouts, and above the trail heads. Who could not have been impressed? Obviously it mattered deeply that the jammers were not exhibits—visitors delighted that they were real. The absence of such an unusual survivor as the jammer would have made a difference in how visitors approached this park.

At last we had turned noticeably upward, the road hugging the sharpening cliffs. Ahead lay the high point, both literally and figuratively, of a visit to Glacier National Park. "This is Going-to-the-Sun Road," our driver repeated several times, obviously in love with the sound of it. We should remain seated and keep our arms in. There was no need to stand anyway now that we were walled in by mountain glory on every side.

At Logan Pass, we got to stretch our legs and learn more about the highway. Fortunately, its architects and engineers had been deeply inspired by the legacy of the progressives and the Great Northern Railway.[7] Upheld by the desire for change but avoiding unwanted change, the results were indeed striking.

It explained further why after all these years Glacier's ambiance remained unique. Few other parks had preserved the consistency in asking visitors for restraint. Going-to-the-Sun Road restricted the size of vehicles; the humility of the jammers remained everyone's guide. The road had not been widened and straightened just to make room for speed. In Glacier, cars and motor homes gave way to the natural resources and not the other way around. At every stage in Glacier's development, responsible decision making influenced the future, respecting the park's landscape, wildlife, and visitors. Resisting change for the sake of consumerism, park managers had determined to honor their historical mandate.

Even as we returned to the hotel, the lesson was repeated. We had enjoyed each other's company so much that we agreed to meet for dinner. Rather than disrupt our conversation in the meantime, we allowed ourselves to be sidetracked by the lobby. After dinner we were back on our chairs and sofas, conversing deep into the night. Historically, public spaces had been all about what we were doing now. As the designers of yesteryear had intended, the lobby had brought us close, and then brought us closure. Upon leaving Glacier, we might well believe in the same mandate for every landscape.[8]

Now regretting my own departure, I planned my remaining day in the wilderness. It should be another hike, I decided, choosing to circle Two Medicine Lake. It too had been a historical favorite with railroad visitors, promoted heavily by the Great Northern Railway. Now that Glacier was nearing the end of the season, the jammers had dropped the route—I would need to rent a car. The station had a rental counter, and because it was September, I was quickly signed out and on my way.

Although I reveled in Two Medicine Lake, I missed the charm of the day before. I missed the jammers and my newfound friends. Solitude is wonderful, my hike reaffirmed, but preservation is about consensus. I walked the lake with that thought, ignoring the posted warnings of a grizzly sighting. (This was stupid, I now confess—no one should ignore that warning.) If we have wilderness, it is because we have agreed to have it. No one gets solitude without a community that establishes and protects the public lands. In affirming the national parks, the *Empire Builder* and Glacier's built environment had affirmed our need to discuss these issues. It was a discussion impossible to have on a highway or at the airport in nearby Kalispell.

Glacier's legacy was in honoring the opportunity to draw Americans close. All day I tingled at the possibility of sighting a grizzly in the wild, and yet was just as delighted to recall the days before when, on the edge of wilderness, I was part of the community learning to save it.

At dusk I returned eagerly to that community and found it finally changed. The melancholy drifting down the mountainsides was closing in at the lodge as well. In the lobby, just yesterday so bright and cheerful, a palpable sadness hung in the air. A growing group of seasonal workers was leaving with me on the eastbound train. Within days most would be back at college. East Glacier Park Lodge was closing; the season's benediction was at hand. Time to go, another train was saying, and none of the staff was happy.

Next morning, the need to rise in the dark for a dawn departure only added to the gloom. On the station platform, the ritual had begun—hugs and handshakes, more exchanging of addresses and phone numbers, and a constant wiping away of tears. Summer had gone by too quickly, and there was no way to get it back. The few staying to close the lodge had a brief reprieve, but one without their friends.

At least Glacier, I observed, had its ritual—its history was still marvelously intact. What if these young people had not had this togetherness? Everywhere else on the edge of parks—at Gardiner, West Yellowstone, El

Portal, Canyon Depot, and Cedar City—end-of-season had come to mean just departure, closure shattered into bits and pieces. Tears shed at leaving Glacier formed the bonds of knowing why Glacier must be saved.

Then it was here, the end of the season, down to a final bend of track. The train was quickly off the curve and pulling in. Boarding among the last crescendo of good-byes, I was looking forward to a special hello. In the excitement, I had almost forgotten my pledge to reunite with the doctor and his wife—we had agreed to meet in the dining car after final call for breakfast.

However, I sensed the tension too. When would any of us come this way again? Or would we ever repeat the journey? In case not, I needed to etch Glacier into my memory just as much as these students did. Then we were moving, trees flashing past the windows, and the summer had truly ended. I glanced back, saw the last brave smiles, and just then the sunlight crowned the mountains.

What a place and what a lesson for these young people to be carrying home. Neither time nor distance (as history points out) could erase the wonders these lives had touched, nor erase their own achievement either. These were the young people who had stuck it out. In Yellowstone, they had historically been known as the "savages," in Yosemite, the "Curry coolies." These were the seasonal workers, the two-dollars-an-hour crowd, who every year rebuilt a park's community and then, returning to their colleges and universities, taught its values there. The date of their departure said it all. They had honored their contracts to the letter. Not only had they promised their best, but they had also given their best, right up to summer's end.

Now I joined them in pressing against the windows, watching the Rockies fall quickly behind. Finally, someone broke the silence, asking the question on everyone's mind: "Are you coming back next summer?" "You bet I am!" "Me, too!" Sobs died instantly in the collective realization that trains do go the other way.

The *Empire Builder* would defend the need and the goal so long as they were here. These young people probably knew little about progressivism, but certainly they had learned what Glacier meant. Out of the intensity of their current sadness would grow the durability of their lifetime gift. This summer would always be special and they special with it, having lived the wonder of preservation taught by the *Empire Builder* and Glacier National Park.

Grand Canyon

In perhaps their greatest fight of the 1960s, environmentalists defended Grand Canyon National Park. The U.S. Bureau of Reclamation was proposing to dam the Colorado River immediately above and below the park for hydroelectric power and water storage. The flood pool of the lower reservoir would back up for miles into the park; the upper reservoir, in Marble Canyon, would inundate another pristine wilderness. David Brower, the embattled director of the Sierra Club, bitterly concluded, "If we can't save the Grand Canyon, what the hell can we save?"[1]

Fortunately, Congress came to its senses, and the Grand Canyon was spared the dams. As a final gesture before leaving office on January 20, 1969, President Lyndon Johnson proclaimed Marble Canyon a national monument.[2] But environmentalists took little note of the opportunity that had been lost along the rim. While the dams were stirring a fire-storm of protest, the canyon's historic railroad quietly died. Where the issue was access for the automobile, environmentalists could be just as forgetful and contradictory as any citizen.

Environmentalists always seemed to be hoping against all odds that the problem would just disappear, that all those visitors and all those cars would simply go somewhere else. Or the same visitors would come to agree with environmentalists that everyone should walk—perhaps 5 or 10 miles in, whatever it took to discourage frivolous visitation.[3]

On a summer day in the mid-1920s, Grand Canyon Depot hosts seven trains and a private car. Each coach carried a minimum of fifty passengers. Today, the three thousand visitors represented here would require an average of twenty cars for each railroad coach and a parking area five times as large as the train yard. Original photograph by Santa Fe Railway. Courtesy of Grand Canyon National Park Museum (image 6590).

That a railroad offered a more reasonable solution barely crossed the movement's mind. Europe's example was also lost on environmentalists still thinking that visitors ought to sacrifice. Of all railroads that had served the national parks, the Grand Canyon Railway was closest to the European model. Inaugurated on September 17, 1901, the 65-mile branch of the Atchison, Topeka & Santa Fe left the main line at Williams, Arizona, ending just 100 yards from the rim.[4] For the United States, this depth of penetration into the wilderness was most unusual; only in Europe did railroads commonly enter protected areas, especially a landscape of such renown.

Acceptance of the European philosophy at the Grand Canyon had been purely accidental. In 1901 the Grand Canyon was not yet a national park, a fact the Santa Fe Railway hoped to change by building the canyon branch. The point is that the railroad still came first. Although this is true of Glacier, the Great Northern Railway only skirted its southern edge. At Grand Canyon, the Santa Fe came in boldly, well past the future park boundary.

Even now that the United States is fully settled and fully paved, Americans do not grasp the lost opportunity. Highways are inside the parks, and railroads are outside. Progressivism, as symbolized in the Grand Canyon Railway, had always sensed the contradiction. In the European style of scarcity, the Grand Canyon Railway restrained everyone's individualism. Observing America's prejudice for land abundance, the highway restored individualism and dismissed restraint. Thus, the highway got to build past the railroad and claim 30 more miles of rim. Railroads could come to the parks, but should never enter the parks—the overlooks should be for cars.

The lost art of progressivism was to ask for consistency. If a railroad was considered a developer in a national park, why was a highway not a developer, too? A highway is more permanent. To remove a railroad is simply reversing the process of laying rails and ties. Yet when the nation made its choice for preservation, railroads languished at the gates. Every taste of wilderness would come with rubber.

Americans making the choice for wilderness had simply picked which illusion they preferred to accompany it. Conveniently, the heavy industry—steel mills, factories, and refineries—that the automobile depended on was farther out of sight. On the other hand, a train, as a self-contained community, was very much in sight. Visitors entering the parks by railroad just *had* to be more invasive. A locomotive—steaming, belching, hissing—looked like industry, so obviously, the railroad did not belong.

Few Americans could see that the automobile belonged even less, and indeed, my family initially was right there with them. We too first visited the national parks by car, never thinking (at least at the time) that it was a problem. Arriving on the South Rim of the Grand Canyon in August 1959, we delighted in another campground choked with motor vehicles. We drove everywhere looking for groceries, ice cream, and souvenirs. We toured both highways along the rim, never considering railroads, as Europeans would have.

Indeed, the Park Service itself never mentioned them. None of the campfire lectures we attended mentioned that Grand Canyon was originally a railroad park. I recall no one telling us that El Tovar, the rustic hotel above Canyon Depot, had been built by the Santa Fe. The comings and goings of the trains delighted me, but no one in uniform pointed them out; rather, the slogan of the day was Mission 66. Coinciding with

The *75th Anniversary Limited,* a special train of the National Parks and Conservation Association, arrives at Grand Canyon Depot on May 12, 1994. The crew gathers to have its picture taken. Photograph by the author.

the fiftieth anniversary of the National Park Service in 1966, Mission 66 promised to banish overcrowding by building even wider roads and larger parking lots.

Few planners seemed to be thinking past 1966. Environmentalists were also caught up in the notion that it all came down to highways. They talked of restricting cars, not eliminating them. At Park Service headquarters, the challenge was still fitting automobiles to the parks, not resolving whether this challenge was legitimate.

In 1980, on my return to South Rim, it was obvious that the highway had won and the railroad lost. The south entrance looked like a tourist trap—hardly what history called a gateway. Strategies used by the Santa Fe Railway to instill wonder now implored the motorist to consume. As early in the trip as a highway back in New Mexico, a rank of billboards had proclaimed, "McDonald's at Grand Canyon." What for the Grand Canyon

Railway had been moderation—a stopping here and a stopping there—had with the highway become envelopment—the right to develop everything.

I took a swing past Canyon Depot, and in the trees sprouting between the tracks found at least a measure of reassurance. Undoubtedly, before anyone could attempt to remove the trees, an environmental impact statement would be required. In government, the process might take forever—meanwhile, the rails would get to stay. I prayed the entire right-of-way was growing trees all the way back to Williams.

To be sure, any investor committed to restoring the Grand Canyon Railway could expect little help from the Park Service—or from Amtrak. Time and again, both had told me that any such restoration would prove unfeasible. Visitation figures told a different story: there were 3 million visitors in 1980. The number of cars alone entering Grand Canyon had passed 1 million.

The dream remained powerful, and finally a group of investors saw it too. Slowly, an agreement to restore the railroad advanced past the talking stage; however, that first group of investors failed. Suddenly it was 1987 and the talk had turned to do or die. A salvage crew rumbled into Williams, this time committed to gutting the line.

Then it came—the miracle. Abruptly, the salvage crew was halted. A Phoenix couple, Max and Thelma Biegert, had determined the railroad could pay its way. They backed the railroad with a substantial fortune, committing millions to rebuild the tracks. Work was started immediately, the Biegerts intent on beginning passenger service by the spring of 1990. Along with track, bridges, and support facilities, the historic Harvey House in downtown Williams would also be restored, as would Canyon Depot below El Tovar. Two steam locomotives confirmed the project's authenticity, along with a dozen period coaches from the 1920s.

Without a doubt, historic preservation was never better served. The larger vision—at times difficult even for the Biegerts—was how to break peoples' umbilical cord to the automobile. As envisioned, the railroad's principal market would be Interstate 40, which passed the railroad's door. In Europe, its principal market would have been the entire continent, with connections to every train. Historically, the canyon branch had provided that connection to the American city without the use of automobiles.

Ultimately, the restoration was a private display of confidence that enough people off Interstate 40 would park and ride. The Biegerts' eagerness to push the inaugural forward had nothing to do with government policy—why wait, they simply decided. Instead of spring 1990, operations would begin September 17, 1989, exactly eighty-eight years—to the day—since the first train to Grand Canyon. Meanwhile, it was hardly the Biegerts' fault that Amtrak refused to acknowledge it. Incredibly, Amtrak would not connect with the Grand Canyon Railway until 1999, ten full years past the restoration.

A further point of preservation was the unfinished agenda of replacing cars entirely. With almost 200,000 riders per year in 2005, the railway was easily displacing 70,000 cars. However, why should the envelopment of the South Rim by automobiles be allowed in any scenario, with the railroad so close at hand? Why not require that every visitor take the train in from Williams?

Similarly, progressive instincts called for a railroad that was not the tail end of a car trip. The decision of what to bring to wilderness should be made at home. Why not give Americans the ability to make the decision in Boston and New York, just as they might for a visit to Zurich, Amsterdam, or Berlin? Why force the Grand Canyon Railway itself to build a larger parking lot? Indeed, their billboards were up from day one. The railroad's historical pledge to the Arizona landscape, not just Grand Canyon, had already lost its punch. The new railroad was bartering with motorists over why they should leave the road.

The Biegerts at least knew they were bartering; the Park Service still refused to admit it. A successful railroad was too much for an agency still married to the car. Suddenly, rangers accused the railroad of being a distraction (as if a road was not); the trains were entertaining, but hardly serious transportation (as if Detroit never sold cars as fun); approaching the rim, the trains blew their whistles and rang their bells (as if cars and buses never blew their horns); the whistles reached into the canyon proper (as if the tourist helicopters circling above the canyon intruded silently).

The double standard could not have been more obvious. As it stood, the most serious threat to natural quiet inside the canyon came from its scores of aircraft. Beginning just after daybreak and continuing until dark, sightseeing planes and helicopters droned overhead. The railroad was in a historical, developed area; the overflights violated actual wilderness.

The Park Service still complained—next at Canyon Depot. All those passengers from the train crossing the highway were forcing people in cars to wait. Although it happened just once a day, that was enough for critics. In an incredible feat of illogic, they protested that, in a national park, people on foot were a nuisance.

It remained a matter of invention driving legitimacy: what the Park Service preferred over what it professed. The Park Service forgave all who invaded wilderness so long as the invader came by car. What should Americans want from the Grand Canyon Railway, if not final release from such double standards?

This painting, commissioned by the Grand Canyon Railway, suggests what the rim of Grand Canyon would look like without cars. Reminiscent of Europe, light-rail transit and bicycles adapt easily to the existing road. J. Craig Thorpe, *Preservation Restored*, 1996. Oil on canvas, 16 x 20 inches. Used by permission of the artist.

In other words, where should park-and-ride begin? Waiting until the edge of wilderness, the car was still poised to make demands of it. In 1994 I asked if the Grand Canyon Railway would allow me an experiment. In celebration of its seventy-fifth anniversary, the National Parks and Conservation Association (NPCA) had accepted my proposal to run a special, transcontinental train. Would Grand Canyon Railway smooth the negotiations with both Amtrak and Santa Fe? I asked only for historical integrity—the passengers should get to remain on the train. Arriving at Williams from Chicago, the transfer should be the original one, passing off our entire train from the main line directly to the canyon branch.

NPCA's three-car special departed from Chicago on May 9, 1994, behind Amtrak's *Southwest Chief.* After a stopover at Santa Fe, New Mexico, we arrived at Flagstaff, Arizona, on May 11. There we uncoupled from the *Chief* and continued the last 30 miles to Williams as a separate train.

Thirty-five minutes later, at Williams Junction, we took the historical main line down the hill. Gliding into Williams proper, we were switched immediately to the canyon branch. Not since 1968 had a train carrying paying passengers joined the main line and branch together. The next morning, for the first time in a generation, a bona fide passenger train would link Chicago with the rim of the Grand Canyon at El Tovar.

Now that, I reminded the passengers, was progressivism's idea of park-and-ride: all the way by train. The lessons of the Grand Canyon—of preservation—still ask for that level of connectivity everywhere. It is hardly progressive to impose on the edge of wilderness, just so the car can be appeased. To envelop the parks from without hardly helps to save them from within.

To be sure, there will always be defenders of park-and-ride. However, if stewardship is to flourish, the objective is not to be parking anywhere. At least restoring the Grand Canyon Railway ensures the opportunity. That by itself is a great accomplishment and a reminder, in the land of the automobile, of what it will take to restore our parks.

Future
Imperfect

If the passenger train has a disadvantage, it would have to be lack of speed—not actual speed, but potential speed that people believe will one day be achieved. No barrier has proved more formidable in explaining the absence of trains today. Indeed, it remains the perfect excuse: the best trains are yet to be, so why waste resources building trains today that will be obsolete tomorrow? Imagine train travel without any rails, perhaps by magnetic levitation. In that case, the railroad would need a guideway with pillars set in the ground. Imagine going 300 mph! Other futurists predict bullet trains with jet engines; still others, tunnels bored beneath the continent. Trains underground would take advantage of a giant vacuum. The common vision is obvious—the quest for greater and greater speeds. Face it, proponents argue, Americans have always loved going fast.[1]

The problem is that the moment futurists ask the impossible, they force the nation to consider it probable. In effect, the future becomes a dumping ground. Futurists may not wish to generate delay, but that is exactly how the government interprets it. Oh, good, in the future, trains will be better. We don't have to do anything now. The victim—what is lost—in that scenario is what is attainable now—what is proven and what works. Future possibilities become not a reason to wait for higher standards, but worse, a rationale for accepting delay.

Though speed is the vision, it is not the issue. In cities, cars are slower than they have ever been, yet the nation goes right on building them. Jet aircraft are ten times faster, yet their share in the transportation market averages just 10 percent. For the 90 percent of trips Americans take by car, the average speed is barely that of the passenger train in its heyday. During the streamliner era, beginning in the 1930s, trains regularly exceeded 100 mph. In the vaunted Northeast Corridor, now Amtrak's showcase, the famous GG1 passenger locomotive reached that speed, and higher[2]—and that was seventy years ago.

Cars themselves have barely changed since the 1960s, at least insofar as speed is concerned. However, only the passenger train gets the crippling label of being conventional, as if anything merely current is inherently wasteful. After World War II, the nation heard it stated confidently, with no supporting evidence, that rail technology would be superseded. Many more wonderful things were on the way—supersonic airplanes, fusion power, and regular trips to the moon. Hollywood and science fiction added to the attack on things conventional. Who needed railroads when we could colonize space?[3]

However, the future predicted in the 1950s had fallen apart by the 1970s. After a dozen men had stood on the moon, few Americans talked seriously about colonization. It had taken $24 billion just to put those twelve there. Imagine the cost, asked the human ecologist Garrett Hardin, to colonize the earth's population growth for just a single day.[4] Perhaps the moon could wait.

And what was the point of escaping a living planet for a dead one? If Casey Jones was not Captain Kirk, at least the dream of railroads had been realized. Where it remained a dream of landscape, at least something good might come of it. As early as 1912, the British ambassador to the United States, James Bryce, feared for the future, not of space travel, but rather of spaciousness. Focusing on protecting the beauty of North America, a hypothetical journey was the last thing on his mind. "What Europe is now is that toward which you in America are tending," he warned. "Europe is a populous, overcrowded continent; you will someday be a populous and ultimately perhaps even a crowded continent." Bryce advised that America wisely "take thought at once, before the overcrowding comes on, as to how you will deal with the difficulties which we have had to deal with in Europe, so that you may learn as much as possible from our experience, and not find too late that the beauty and solitude of nature have been snatched from you by private individuals."[5]

Although the United States led the world in the establishment of national parks, the world itself had been circumscribed. Nature was in retreat everywhere. "The surface of this little earth of ours is limited, and we cannot add to it." Its dimensions would not increase, so it followed that "even your scenery is not inexhaustible, and, with your great population and the growing desire to enjoy the beauties of nature, you have not got any more than you need."[6]

Bryce had put the questions back where they belonged: What was the future Americans desired, not merely the future that some predicted? What was the responsible future—indeed, the likely future—not just the enticing one? In a world that would not be getting any larger, why act as if it would?

These ideas were of course ignored, and the automobile won the twentieth century because it was the private way to the future. Speed had little to do with it. Investing billions of dollars in high-speed rail will not resolve that larger issue. Do Americans want a living landscape or, as with going to the moon, is one form of space as good as another?

For all the time Americans spend waiting for a future that never arrives, we might be better to plan a future we could actually live in. Is life better now because someone once predicted the existence of trains we still don't have? What might we be doing with the trains we threw away? Is it the future that fills our emptiness? Where is the future as I wanted it, the restoration of the *Phoebe Snow*? Where is any train home to Binghamton, either conventional or high-speed?

According to the futurists, I am supposed to be delighted that *Phoebe Snow* is gone—that relic from the past, barely making 80 mph. It was just in the way of the future; but futurists have put nothing in its place. By car, I cannot beat *Phoebe*'s former schedule, and I have often done far worse. And what do I get when I try? I get to leave New York City in a barrage of traffic demanding my full attention. Every second, I get to deal with unbridled fanaticism as I enter the battle of constantly weaving cars and trucks. Clear of the city, the fanaticism of the road warriors abates slightly as traffic decreases, but not so as any driver should feel relaxed. Depending on the season, Route 17 is susceptible to a thunderstorm or a snow squall or miles of freezing rain. Suddenly, even the fanaticism of the road warriors is not enough to keep them out of the ditch. There we have

Following pages: The Santa Fe Railway was no stranger to speed. Running fast trains, the company also, in a 1952 series of advertisements, reminded Americans what trains were for. These selections from the series emphasize the wonders to be seen when traveling by train. Author's collection.

THE SATURDAY EVENING POST

Through your magic window

The sights you see on the Santa Fe are
matched by the comforts you enjoy! Everyone
of Santa Fe's five great trains each day, each way,
between Chicago and California is planned, equipped
and staffed to make your trip such fun
you hate to have it end. Ask your ticket agent
or travel agent about the wide choice of schedules
and accommodations available.

PUEBLO INDIANS make interesting
camera subjects when your Santa Fe train
pauses at Albuquerque, New Mexico.

Santa Fe

*Pueblo Indian
Comanche Dancer
—painted by
an Indian artist*

Super Chief · Chief · El Capitan · Grand Canyon · California Ltd.
Texas Chief *between Chicago-Texas*
Kansas City Chief *between Chicago-Kansas City*

R. T. Anderson, General Passenger Traffic Manager, Santa Fe System Lines, Chicago 4, Illinois

139

it—yesterday's tomorrow, our promised future for replacing the *Phoebe Snow*. This is what we got for believing the futurists who claimed the passenger train was too slow.

Futurists had similarly promised that the airplane would never fail, forgetting again it must get off the ground (also that smaller cities, like Binghamton, are forever being dropped by the airlines). My last time leaving La Guardia, we taxied and waited in line for forty minutes. Finally we were airborne, but what more about air travel can be said? It begins at a veritable madhouse called a terminal, now with guards demanding you practically get undressed. "We'll have that belt, sir, and your shoes, please, and your sport coat, if you don't mind." It is usually polite, but it is humiliating. Who would want a future of that?

Is that the future we really chose, or again, simply the future we somehow made? In Europe, a city the size of Binghamton would have several trains every hour. Trains like those originating in the Northeast Corridor would fan out in all directions; trains would not simply die upon arriving at the last station or be turned to repeat the line. If the Northeast Corridor were in Europe, it would be one line among many others. Pursuing a trip home to Binghamton, I could at least make a transfer somewhere. No city would be the end of the line, but rather each city would be a new beginning.

Whether I fly or drive, I miss the meaning of that comparison. I miss the promise of the future now. I would take the *Phoebe Snow* back in a heartbeat, and the landscape and cityscape that came with her. I accept the lesson of the *Phoebe Snow*: sometimes the wisest speed is slowing down.

If there is magnetic levitation in Binghamton's future, it is a future I will not live to see. Besides, what would I get to see, other than a blur outside the window. That would just be a grasp for privacy in a different form, another fixation on goals alone. That would be affectation, not transportation. Similarly, if *Phoebe* is to be sucked through some future tunnel, I would just as soon not live to see that either. The old girl doing 300 mph could not possibly improve on the train and landscape as they were.

It takes no courage to preach a future where speed is the only goal. It should be those other goals that give us pause. In that case, which future would we prefer—the trains we had or those on the drawing board? What satisfaction do we derive from making speed our only future? Even granting futurists that argument—that speed is the future, no matter what—there is still no guarantee that the nation would be happier. Just as likely, we would be bored with the monotony of it all, and would tire of that future too.

The Time We Save

Never at a loss for strong opinions, my mother had no use for retirement. The things people wanted to do in life should never be postponed. So many of her friends had done just that, but upon reaching retirement they had unexpectedly died. Why had they not planned life in reverse, living it to the fullest while they had it? Especially, why had they put off seeing the country? All they had to do was take a train.

Foreign visitors often comment that Americans talk constantly about saving time. Americans act as if time can be saved in a bank. The truth remains that whether used wisely or unwisely, time lost is lost forever. A distinguished writer got the question back to railroads by asking, "And what will we do with the time we save?"

The writer was E. M. Frimbo and his magazine, *The New Yorker*. Frimbo (pen name for Rogers E. M. Whitaker) was delightfully unapologetic: he hoped to die riding trains. Thus, like my mother, if far more eloquently, he questioned how Americans had turned time into a commodity. "And what will we do," he repeated, acknowledging that planes were faster, "with the time we save?"[1]

What Whitaker loved about railroads was their willingness to sell the landscape. Americans should want to see their country—the landscape is education, not a waste of time. Seeing the country is not to misuse it, nor is it misuse to insist that time be spent having fun.

Our final disparagement is that no amount of time spent traveling is short enough. Cross-country or crosstown, five minutes extra can be too much. Landscape pays the price—endless ranks of shopping malls and strip malls importune the motorist to pull over. The irony is that we spend all our time parking, then trudging across the gargantuan lots. We might have walked on a sidewalk and met a neighbor; we might have snatched some joy from life.

Recall, too, the supersonic transport, recently discontinued by British Airways and Air France as too expensive for them to fly. In 1970, when Congress refused to support an American version of the plane, the airlines were incensed. Passengers would have saved three hours flying from coast to coast, they warned. In rebuttal, critics noted that the plan would burn too much fuel and subject the country to daily sonic booms. And so the debate persists for trains. In the Northeast Corridor, Amtrak struggles to save time in increments of ten or fifteen minutes, as if that last increment will motivate a return to trains. Likely, Amtrak would be better off raising confidence in what exists, rather than learn the heard way—as the airlines have—that increments of speed can prove very costly.

Today, with cell phones and laptops, we can be in instant communication anywhere. We have even less reason to be in a hurry than people a hundred years ago—and yet we hurry more. In the United States, we seem to think that the only way we can be sure the traveler has not wasted time is if travel denigrates pleasure and elevates anxiety.

The consequence is going places without ever knowing where one has been. No passenger train ever allowed that. A sense of place always mattered—in the naming of trains, in the naming of cars, indeed, in everything the railroads did. The Pullmans of the *Phoebe Snow* borrowed the Indian place names of New York and Pennsylvania; names like *Tunkhannock* and *Kittatiny* linked the train to history. After two decades of muddling around with numbers, in the 1990s Amtrak returned to the practice, naming its newest sleepers after the fifty states. Amtrak finally got it. People remember names, not numbers. Names have the power of association; time itself is just a number.

Mother had loved the names and avoided the numbers. When she was in her sixties, her favorite number was nine—the number of times she had toured Europe on a rail pass. In 1983 she retired from the Binghamton City School District, having been a secretary there for twenty-three years. But she had not obsessed about her retirement; most of her trips to Europe had come before. When at last she retired, her friends called her back, urging that she run for the school board. She did and won.

In October 1985, preparing to stand for reelection, she received unwelcome news: her breast cancer had returned and spread. After two

Author's mother, Erika Runte, changing trains on the platform of the station at Wiesbaden, Germany. It is her third visit to Europe on a Eurail Pass, June 1982. Photograph by the author.

operations, including a mastectomy, she began chemotherapy in 1987. She was obviously getting tired, so I suggested she come to Seattle where my wife and I could keep an eye on her. She could avoid the cold of the approaching winter. Besides, Seattle is famous for treating cancer.

I knew she would accept; I was simply taken aback by her choice of travel. "Alfred," she announced cheerfully over the phone, "I have decided to take the train." She had barely said it before I protested. She would be by herself for three days. She would have to get on the train in Syracuse, two hours from Binghamton by bus. "I think it would be better if you flew," I argued. Too late, she had already bought her ticket—the *Lake Shore Limited* from Syracuse to Chicago, then the *Empire Builder* to Seattle. I was not to worry; she had an economy bedroom from Chicago. She assured me she would be just fine.

I still tried to talk her out of it, reminding her she needed to keep up with her chemotherapy. No problem: her doctors had told her to plan her next treatment after New Year's. That was the part still troubling me; her diagnosis had seemed more urgent. I still stumbled to find the words. "Think of the time," I finally protested. "Alfred," her voice went cold, "I am past thinking about only time."

I knew she had won the argument. When she visited Seattle in 1980, she had flown, and reminded me she hadn't seen a thing. Three years later she had come by train, choosing the *Canadian* from Toronto to Vancouver. Amtrak served Toronto out of Syracuse, so getting to the *Canadian* had been a breeze. Although the train from Vancouver to Seattle had been discontinued, that leg was only four hours on the bus. She had loved it so much, she repeated the trip in 1984. Now she was reminding me that the *Empire Builder* was one of my favorite trains. Had I not taken it to Glacier a few years ago, she asked? "Ten years ago," I replied, finally conceding her point. "All right, Mom. Just be careful. And call me whenever you can so I know you are okay."

I promised to be waiting at Seattle's King Street Station the morning her train arrived. When she appeared on the platform, I swallowed my relief, and was struck by how good she seemed to feel. Despite the pallor in her face, she bubbled over with enthusiasm. "Alfred, you must say hello to this wonderful person I met yesterday in the lounge car. Her name is Maggie, and I told her to look for us by checked baggage." The next moment Mother had taken me by the arm and hustled me off in that direction.

Maggie, I soon learned, was a receptionist at the University of Minnesota. As they recounted the highlights of their trip for me, I could tell they had ensconced themselves in the lounge. I could see them there, chattering happily, stealing glimpses of the plains and mountains. Obviously, the discrepancy in their ages had made no difference—each had discovered a kindred spirit. Two weeks later Maggie wrote, "Thanks again for being such a friend on the trip out. I hope we meet again!"

By then Mother had taken a turn for the worse, and I was beginning to understand: the *Empire Builder* had been her hope for normalcy, delighting one last time in the power of expectation. She had found this in her experience on the train, in Maggie and the landscape most of all. Her decision to ride the train announced with gentleness that she believed her last moments to be few. I am so grateful I failed to talk her out of the ride. After all, it was Mom who had won Cinderella Weekend three times, believing her friends and family deserved the *Phoebe Snow*.

Something Real

Beyond arguments about the future and saving time, there is a belief creeping into American culture that authenticity is what we make of it—that authenticity can be contrived. Historically, trains authentic to the American experience did not pander or play a role. All travel was considered serious, whether for business or enjoyment. Now, many trains no longer run on a schedule—they just have a script. Travel is a series of sound bites. As long as a train's appearances are true to form, that is the only reality a passenger needs.

Today, new promoters are selling the passenger train as a theme park. Fake is as good as real, as long as the fakery comes with a theme. Now that theme parks can supply any meaning, they may substitute for travel too. Bored? There is always another theme park; just keep looking and find the theme you like. Disneyland, Six Flags, Busch Gardens, and Sea World—even the so-called reality shows on television—are but a few examples of the increase in number and range of theme parks in our nation. People look for meaning in what is not real, as if what is actually real cannot compete.

In railroads, although the theme train may not run in an oval, there is still no question it is contrived. Consider the growth of excursion trains, dinner trains, and trains that claim to "cruise." Many of the passenger train's strongest critics believe that such theme trains should take over long-distance markets. For that dwindling number of people willing to ride a train all day (and able to afford it), virtual reality is good enough. Scheduled trains are money losers the country can no longer afford.[1]

The sacrifice of purpose makes the sacrifice of trains easier. The hidden danger of losing authenticity is the diversity that gets replaced. Diversity is not just about race or gender—that definition is often a contrivance too. To embrace diversity in the context of travel is, rather, to agree that we are a better people, both individually and collectively, the more we get to mingle. The more we talk and the more we share, the more we find in common. Historically, these experiences were possible because trains were common carriers—they stopped to pick up everyone. Theme parks, much like theme trains, contribute to someone's bottom line, but that is about business, not about strengthening the culture. Trains have always been about both of these.

Limiting long-distance train travel to those with the largest pocketbooks would be the ultimate retreat from the meaning of travel. Granted, wealth has its privileges, even on a passenger train: there have always been luxury Pullman and economy coach. Most airlines still have first-class seating. However, the nation has never risked the obscenity that a common carrier is *all* about price and privilege. On most trains, the dining car remained open to everyone, so Pullman passengers mingled with those from coach. It is that larger meaning of common carrier—democracy—that privilege seekers would now replace.

Legitimate travelers, the familiar argument reasserts itself, are those whose purpose is economic. Allowing more excursions would free Amtrak to address the priorities of the business traveler. If people want to see the country—"just" run around—they should be pleased to pay some operator other than Amtrak. Freeing it of all those purposeless travelers would allow Amtrak to get back down to business.

Inevitably, the competition just as easily makes the argument that train travel itself is frivolous. Business travelers could be (and should be) taking a car or an airplane. No one sees the insidious side of the argument that suggests trains should not even be an option. Come that winter day when choices one and two aren't moving, choice three will be grounded too—not by weather, but by prejudice.

So what if I am having *fun* riding a common carrier? Let's put it to the congressional delegation from Nevada. Just because Reno and Las Vegas are all about having fun, does the nation get to close your airports? Are these cities not at least as frivolous as a long-distance train? Sure, Las Vegas may be a crowning achievement—an entire city with theme-park status. But Nevada describes its tourism as an *industry*, as does every state. If that term can be applied to tourism, why not apply it to trains?

When Las Vegas stripped Truxton and Crozier Canyons in nearby Arizona of decorative rocks, it defended its actions as business. But when the Santa Fe Railway protected those canyons, introducing them to passengers, how was that considered frivolous in any way? There lies the end result of such arguments—more attacks on the American land. As it was for Gaviota, Azilum, and Wyalusing Rocks, this end result encourages the passenger train to not be a common carrier.

Travel, needing always to defend itself as a business, disallows other meanings. Under the promotional guidance of the Santa Fe, the canyons along its right-of-way were sold as scenery. Las Vegas could not care less. The city markets the Grand Canyon through aerial tours, but as a theme park, not as a national park. The Santa Fe Railway instructed its passengers to linger, savoring the canyon for days or weeks. The Santa Fe could have succumbed just as easily, herding people into the Grand Canyon and herding them out. The point is that, unlike an airplane, a passenger train acts as a steward—unless we resort to fakery and allow only passenger trains that emulate theme parks.

The passenger train ennobles us; the plane just gets us there. Certainly the last train of my mother's life honored her right to face her destiny. It was not a time for fakery, for plastic cups and plastic smiles. It was not a time to fly over a national park, but rather to really *see* one. She could count on the *Empire Builder* to give her truth. It stopped in the working towns and cities of America and welcomed all on board. Maggie's companionship was not an act. That day—and every day—the *Empire Builder* reached for an America that was lovingly real.

The first casualty of an excursion is that feeling of reality. The moment the tour leader is introduced, the travel experience follows a script. Genuine conversation sags, lest someone talking about real issues offend the other passengers. Recall Ricardo Montalban's line on Fantasy Island: "Smiles, everyone." When people are paying for a fantasy, reality is the last thing they want.

The fantasy never gets past inflating every conversation into pure compliance. People daring to flirt with serious conversation are drawn back into "did you see this or that." The staff itself will have been carefully instructed not to butt in and cause "controversy"—these people are your meal ticket, not your friends; we would not want them choosing another theme or, worse for you, not leaving a tip. Only if something goes wrong—and the facade cannot help unraveling—is the humanity shared by the crew and passengers revealed.

The point is not to get the history wrong. There are many wonderful excursions and wonderful people taking them, but travel off common carriers is not the same. Theme parks are not real parks. Modern culture seems to have enough contrivances without forcing them on our trains.

Europe still has the best of both; there are excursion trains and popular luxury trains, but not at the expense of the thousands of trains designed for everyone. There are student passes and senior passes, and second class seating for those on budgets. Excursion trains are considered additions to the service, not substitutes. It is that proposed status here—excursions substituting for common carriers—that leaves a bad taste in the mouth of democracy.

Tour companies that pride themselves on authenticity have noted the problem too. In the absence of true cultural diversity, they at least put a premium on education. Guides are highly trained and are there to inform, not just to entertain. A patronizing tone is out; the obvious is not inflated. Passengers are not served a running commentary that beautiful scenery is obviously beautiful. Serious interpretation, given to meaning and explanation, ensures that even an excursion may rise to purpose.

With that conviction, T. C. Swartz of TCS Expeditions, Seattle, approached me in 1995, asking me to contribute historical commentary by lecturing about the national parks and railroads aboard the *American Orient Express,* his luxury train. Obviously, Swartz wanted the train to be authentic, evoking travel as discovery. Observing the promise, we followed the National Parks and Conservation Association into Grand Canyon National Park, cementing their precedent from the year before of running a special train. The truth of the past had been maintained. The *American Orient Express* asked genuinely for preservation rather than park-and-ride.

In short, Swartz had done his homework, allying immediately with progressive thinking. A profit that grows responsibly should never come at the expense of parks or landscape. Even so, the growing pains proved enormous. Amtrak still held all national rights, so it had to run the train. The railroads were no more cooperative just because so-called influential passengers were on board. And there was still no guarantee that their train would arrive on time. In fact, the *American Orient Express* ran hours late on my first trip, costing us our entire day in New Orleans. The problem was Amtrak's scheduling (despite appearances), and the railroads still called the shots. Luxury was some compensation—but never full compensation—for denying passengers their promised stops.

The problems of railroad culture also remained. Many at Amtrak opposed the *American Orient Express* because it did not pay union wages. Arriving in Los Angeles, the train was purposely delayed in the yards. The railroads were no less opposed to another passenger train that hindered freight. Consequently, on arriving in El Paso, we sat while the freight trains went ahead. Amtrak and the railroads gladly took Swartz's money, but again gave him no guarantees. Inevitably, his frustration built to the point where he decided to part with the *American Orient Express*.

My last assignment with the new owner included Yellowstone and Grand Teton National Parks. Unfortunately, the passengers' orientation no longer stressed a purpose, and their cynicism grabbed the reins. As I proceeded with my commentary, I met resistance even to history. One passenger protested that the federal government should not have established the national parks, nor should the taxpayers be forced to maintain them now. As necessary, the parks should be turned over to legitimate businesses, "who know how to run these things at a profit." The Disney Company came to mind. As if on cue, other passengers began chiming in that my view of the national parks was not objective.

Regardless, it was history's view, I reminded them. The parks belonged to every American. I managed to find a couple of allies, but it was obvious: I was not on script. As the man who had started it all was saying, "we paid for a trip to ride the train—the last thing we need is you, Mr. Runte, ranting and raving about con-ser-va-tion!"

Aboard a common carrier, the discussion need not have ended there. Not every passenger would have thought the same, and many would have asked with me, if you believe that Yellowstone should be like Disneyland, why did you even come? Instead, a censorship of wealth prevailed. The artificiality of materialism censored the discussion, and by silencing history, no one learned a thing.

I tried salvaging the history as best I could, favoring now the passengers' prejudices. Granted, Yellowstone was public land, but the concessionaires were private enterprise. It was not Walt Disney, perhaps, but government had respected the rights of business. As a matter of fact, the concessions traced their origins back to the railroads. The bulk of profits went to the operators, not the government, and the operators payed just a franchise fee.

Then what about snowmobiles, another passenger asked? He had heard they would be banned. If Yellowstone were properly in the hands of private enterprise, no concessionaire would be doing that.

I reminded him that a good-faith effort had been made. For years, the National Park Service had bent over backwards to allow snowmobiles in the park; now that they numbered in the tens of thousands, the mistake was finally obvious. Snowmobiles released many times the level of contaminants of cars in the summer months, and maintaining the roads for snowmobiles cost three to four times more. Patrolling the park in winter had proved another excessive cost. Because winter visitors were more demanding, they disproportionately affected the entire park.

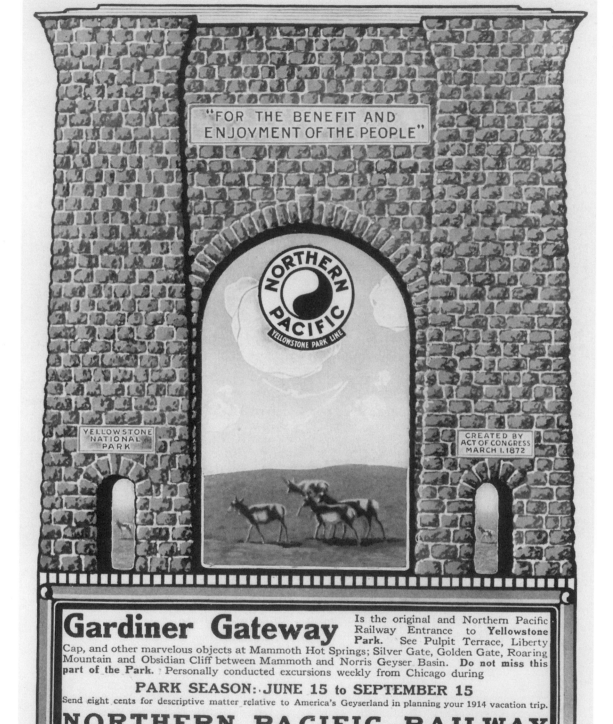

Meanwhile, the needs of preservation had in no way changed. Wildlife needed a season for rest and recuperation, time away from people and their machines. Winter was the season of greatest stress. Animals not in hibernation had to constantly search for food. Historically, tourists had come in summer only, leaving wildlife three seasons to recuperate. Now that every season in Yellowstone had been commercialized, the animals were paying the greatest price.

"So what," my critic retorted, "parks are for people, are they not?" The Constitution was all that mattered here, and his reading of it guaranteed his right to snowmobiles. If he could afford to buy a snowmobile, he had the right to use it—anywhere. He allowed that the National Park Service might charge him extra to defray the extra costs, and he would gladly pay his share of the damage, including his share of the extra patrols. Otherwise, as long as he paid his way, the government should get out of the way. As long as Yellowstone was public land, government had no business telling him what to do.

Finally, the script demanded that I agree. We were at the point in an excursion when the guide agrees to keep his mouth shut. I had made my points, the customers theirs. Technically, I was an employee of the *American Orient Express,* and the customer is always right. Now I was supposed to be Ricardo Montalban: "Smiles, everyone." Thank you, folks, I had never thought of selfishness that way before. Now, look over there in the meadow and tell me: is that a deer?

It was the excursion way, but it was not my way. I agreed with T. C. Swartz: it was time to go. It may be the customer who is always right, but it is the citizen the trains need to serve. An artifice relies on censorship because it cannot possibly survive spontaneity—spontaneity is filled with truth. The truth of citizenship demands plain speaking; an artifice attempts to muzzle it. Especially in a public space as grand as Yellowstone, the public's lips should never be sealed.

The trains of the past had been public spaces, full of serendipity, not just a wine list. I had wished my passengers could have the historical

A younger America respected the national parks as a common good, a philosophy embraced by the railroads. Dedicated in 1903 by President Theodore Roosevelt, the entrance arch at Gardiner Gateway, Yellowstone National Park, proclaims boldly: "For the benefit and enjoyment of the people." The lesson here remains, if the national parks were privatized and commercialized, would we even remember what we have lost? Northern Pacific Railway advertisement, 1914. Author's collection.

experience—a university of the rails. Any train true to history would insist on stewardship and, yes, a belief in the national parks. My disappointment was democracy's own. Where was the idealism that had built our country? Where was our conviction that our national parks were part of our identity? Without preserving these treasured gems of space and beauty, how could we prove to Europe that America had a future they should envy? Individuals who could not possibly want for anything material for themselves begrudged their country its greatest dream.

I was all the more thankful for the trains of history. Even Amtrak, for all its problems, still offered wonder and learning to every citizen. The trains of history—coach or Pullman—had taught every American to believe in the common good. Saying good-bye to the *American Orient Express,* I respected as never before the common carriers. I hoped to reunite with a few trains that still were building America, those encouraging life to stay warm and authentic and noble.

Power and Obligation

If America's dark secret about rail passenger service is that the railroads will never restore it willingly, the inescapable fact is that someone must. The continuing impasse is due to America's penchant for resisting this restoration by tinkering with labels. Historically, even when the railroads were taking public land and money, they agreed only grudgingly that they were utilities. But they are utilities—public thoroughfares—originally chartered by Congress and the states.

Throughout their history, railroads have tried their hardest to make the public forget this. They, like practically every corporation, prefer the term "private enterprise." A utility has no choice but to serve the public; its very character speaks the necessity. However, if people keep asking questions, there is always the label "socialist."

It is this merry-go-round of American history that still muddles the restoration of the passenger train. All arguments become like the question of the chicken and the egg. What started the decline of railroads? Is the fault corporate or is it cultural? What do existing railroads owe the public for any benefits they received in the past? The critic who blames everything on Amtrak is also likely to forget the original problem—the railroads, never wanting Amtrak either, were out to rid themselves of the passenger train. The apologist absolving the railroads of that duplicity notes what the government poured into roads and airlines. A piece of the truth becomes the whole truth. That is how Americans have learned to argue railroad history: the problem is with you, not me.

These days, corporations would like us to believe they have no obligations other than to their stockholders. They claim that when corporations prosper, it trickles down; society gets its benefits in that way. Allowing the railroads that argument in 1970 got the nation Amtrak and the virtual death of the passenger train. The first thing the railroads denied was that the deal was permanent—and so they continue to deny it now. Amtrak was money down on the demise of the passenger train. Its survival was not meant to be permanent.[1]

The trouble was that the public had not been told this. The public believed in the deal—maybe they would not always ride the trains, but they would still have them, just like having the national parks. When comparing Yellowstone to Disneyland, much like the comparison between Amtrak and the airlines, anyone could make the case for dismantling Yellowstone—Disneyland has ten times the patrons. It is this constant harping about who has the numbers that confounds the argument of why the passenger train does not exist. It has to exist before it can exist. If there are fewer trains, there will be fewer passengers. Some parts of the country have no train at all, so how could there be passengers? In 1915, nearing its fiftieth birthday, even Yellowstone had only 51,895 visitors—and the railroads were fighting for every one. Five railroads split 44,447 of those visitors among them.[2]

Numbers do not always tell the story of what the public wants and what makes a profit. When railroads were the only means across the continent, they were pleased with the passengers they had. When they had to compete for passengers, they fell back on their subliminal disgust, reasserting that the passenger was not as profitable. As long ago as the 1890s, James J. Hill, as builder of the Great Northern Railway, likened the passenger train to a male breast—it might look good but it was useless, at least for a railroad's bottom line.[3]

Unfortunately, railroads never got past their own history of when they were the only act in town. Bouts of innovation and industrial design were separated by long periods of indifferent service; railroads procrastinated as long as they could. The more defending delay became the style of management, the more the arrogance of defending it became ingrained in railroad culture. It is that arrogance the public still hears.

In reminding Americans what they owe as the price of citizenship, history reminds corporations that they owe it too. If the experts are right about Social Security, the future is abundantly clear: America cannot afford to keep rebuilding its infrastructure just to keep pace with people's changing preferences. Like it or not, the railroads are part of an infrastructure that the nation desperately needs again.

Is it socialism to force railroads to acknowledge their obligation? No, it is civilization. Such labeling is a dodge meant to evade the responsibility. The label is there to arouse everyone's emotions in the hopes they will not think. Whether you are socialist, capitalist, or communist, the fact is that railroads are utilities. All countries need utilities, regardless of what they call their governments.

In the United States, when utilities are government regulated, the public does not call it socialism, but likely the utilities do. It is the utilities that prefer no regulation. It is the corporations that equate regulation with inefficiency, hoping to escape it. Regulation does not hold a utility hostage; rather, it holds it accountable. We know this and yet continue to be fooled.

When Europe faced the question of how to govern railroads, it nationalized them on the spot; this just meant they dropped the pretense that railroads were not utilities. The role of railroads did not change. In 1978 the federal government dropped virtually all regulation of the airlines, and look at the mess that resulted. It is fine to talk about deregulation until the public starts getting hurt.

Among the railroads, getting back to an understanding of obligation is a decision that must be made, not just an issue of labeling. It is often proposed that the tracks be nationalized, allowing anyone to use them. This is the system used for our highways now. Are truckers calling it socialism? Are automobile owners complaining? The federal government might build and maintain the roadbeds in exchange for fuel taxes and users' fees. In that respect, the rail system would be no different from our highway system: corporate access and public ownership.

It is the schizophrenia, the constant indecision, that makes these decisions appear so difficult. The end result is that everything about railroads in the United States appears hopelessly out of date. The public tunes out the rancor and returns to using cars.

A culture confident in its purposes and definitions would have saved the passenger train long ago—which is precisely why Europe still has good trains. It has both private and nationalized systems; indeed, some have always been private, especially tourist railroads. Other countries, notably Britain, are in the process of restoring railroads to private ownership. What Europe has never lacked is the conviction that railroads are utilities. Within that framework, Europe is pleased to try any experiment and adopt any system, so long as its people are fully served.[4]

It is the sheer unreasonableness of arguing the opposite that keeps America foundering in pointless arguments. No European country would stand for a railroad arguing that a single passenger train disrupts the railroad. In Europe, frequency is the norm—except in the smallest markets, travelers may arrive confidently at any station without needing to check a schedule. The first train out in your direction may not be the fastest or the most convenient, but it is guaranteed to get you started and promise appropriate opportunities to transfer later on.

In the United States, main-line capacity is reserved for freight. Even railroads that agree to run commuter trains still find those terms advantageous. Insisting that government should rebuild the tracks for commuters, the railroads are really hoping to erase bottlenecks for freight. Not a bad exchange for accepting, at the most, a couple dozen commuter trains. But if the government and the public ask for more, the historical roadblocks will be back in place. What the railroads and the public mean by service is still miles apart.

It is not that the railroads have reformed their culture; rather, it is that they have lined up to take advantage of subsidies. The railroads sense that making modest allowances for passengers is a way to expand freight capacity at government expense. But their prejudice is still with freight—they want bigger trains and heavier cars no matter what that means for passengers. The railroads want the public's cash and aid but at the same time continue to deny that they are utilities.[5]

Perversely, the situation explains the sense of urgency among rail passenger activists who argue for dedicated, high-speed lines. Because the railroads resist high-speed service, the need for segregation feeds on itself. Yet again, there would no need for segregation if the railroads would cooperate; as in Europe, what already exists might be improved, rather than having to build entirely new railroad systems.

Granted, existing railroads do not necessarily follow the straightest route, but straightening them would be far cheaper than building lines that are entirely new. Elevated tracks pose other problems, including visual blight. Railroads built down the center of freeways can be eyesores, and buried tracks require excavation, another huge expense.

Besides, all of these options segregate the passenger from where the passenger needs to be—participating in land and life. Complete separation

That railroads can be mindful of their obligations to society is stunningly portrayed in this ad. Although the year was 1966 and rail passenger service everywhere was declining, the Santa Fe Railway remained a noble holdout, talking about the passenger train as a national teacher. Author's collection.

It can't write.
It can't read.
It doesn't have a degree.
It never went to school.
But after books, it's one of the best teachers of American history.

What is it? A big air-conditioned high-level car on the Santa Fe! An enthralling teacher that really carries you away!

Look: Outside its wide windows the whole exciting story of the Wild West unreels. Live. In color:

The Mississippi. Kansas City . . . where the storied Santa Fe Trail begins and the great plains sweep on to Dodge City.

Now, on the horizon, the Rocky Mountains loom. Over Raton Pass, where pony expresses rode hard, we enter the old Spanish and Indian country. Haciendas. Pueblos. Apaches. (*Geronimo!*)

And so to California—the Spanish missions, the Golden Gate, Hollywood, Disneyland!

Your Discover America trip on Santa Fe is an exciting "lesson" 2,000 miles long. And it's waiting for you now on the Super Chief, El Capitan, The Chief, San Francisco Chief, Texas Chief.

Santa Fe

Write Dept. A., Room 333, 80 East Jackson Blvd., Chicago, Ill. 60604 for folders about famous Santa Fe trains or see your nearest ticket agent or travel agent.

of freight and passenger service is beyond the nation's pocketbook, besides being in nobody's best interest. Europe admitted the same limitations early, looking for ways to improve the original railroad system. Where possible, high-speed lines are improvements to existing lines. It is as much an effort to preserve the landscape as it is to improve the trains.

In the United States, these incremental improvements to existing rights-of-way rarely happened because the railroads wished to downsize. Most began by downgrading even their best conventional tracks for slower and heavier freight trains, eliminating the possibility of maintaining speeds, let alone improving them. It is this problem that must be solved. Zipping between Los Angeles and Las Vegas at 200 mph is beside the point. It is only because the federal government owns most of the desert that we keep hearing of such wild-eyed schemes—condemnation costs would be lower.

Europe knows that to condemn land can be prohibitively expensive—and so it has planned more deliberately. While taking the train with my mother through Basel, Switzerland, we were discussing European land use. Overhearing our conversation, the conductor asked permission to interject. He told us that a wealthy developer from the United States had recently purchased an onion field on Basel's outskirts. When the developer took his plans for a housing tract to the authorities, they flatly turned him down. "It is my land," he had protested. "Yes, but it is our country," they reminded him.

The conductor observed that developers in the United States always get the zoning changed, and if that fails, they accuse the authorities of socialism. In Switzerland, social obligation is a permanent part of the cultural mind-set. The field had been in agriculture for six hundred years; the new owner was obligated to honor the original use no less than his predecessors.

In Europe, public transportation slips easily into that give-and-take, into that mind-set of obligation. Of course, not every field in Europe is preserved and not every city has the trains of Paris. But American culture denies the entire concept of obligation. The incentive here is always profit; excelling without it is not to excel. Obligation gets immediately back to the payoff. Recall Amtrak's experience with incentive payments, the so-called bonuses to the railroads if they would operate the trains on time. It is an American argument, hardly a universal one, to insist that responsibility must be bought and that paying once is not enough.

Americans insist on the right to distinguish between citizenship and doing business. I give money to charity, why should I give anything else? Corporations would prefer to publicize their contributions—and separate them from daily responsibility to the culture. American's style of philanthropy is still to distinguish between what one does and what one gives. People give money to charity and think they don't need to give anything else. America's social conscience, which once demanded building communities, now stops after we write a check.

Can we build—do we dare build—obligation back into what we do? Dare we remind our railroads, and ourselves, that giving to charity is only part of it? No doubt, it is wonderful that the railroads commemorate their history with special trains, but why should it end there? Why not insist that the passenger train be a daily obligation rather than just a weekend thing?

The historical arrangement between Amtrak and the railroads only substantiates Europe's argument. Only now that Europe believes obligation to be ingrained in the social fabric have some countries recommitted to private railroads. But most of those arrangements still offer government subsidies until the promised profits materialize. Europe has already prepared itself: if privatization backfires, obligation to the culture still remains. European history has produced a culture of obligation.

Because the history of the United States is wealth, the culture ignores obligation across the board. If profit conquered and built the nation, why can profit not endlessly save and restore it now? Dispensing with the labels once again—socialism, capitalism, and all the rest—history proposes that America is about to change as we make choices in response to an increasing scarcity of natural resources. In making decisions about transportation—which Europe does so well and we so poorly—dare we consider that profit should not be the reason for our decisions, but that obligation should be the reason?

Whatever model we might choose for the passenger train—whether private, nationalized, or some combination of the two—it will not succeed without a cultural belief in the need for passenger service. The stumbling block is not the system, but the lack of a clear mission.

An effective government knows it must preserve what is essential and somehow finds a way to do this. In a civilized society, the future is led by its people's understanding of mutual obligations. In American society, our railroads must be a part of that future.

chapter 17

Rethinking Europe

What if Americans from now on debated railroads without the labeling—without the subliminal negativity that comes with words like subsidy and nationalization? What if the nation focused more on determining what goals were desirable than on what the mechanism to achieve those goals might be called? What if Americans decided to make trains happen rather than allowing the past to trap us in a cultural stranglehold?

How then would we begin? Our goal should not be perfection at some point in the future, constantly belittling what we could have today on the excuse that we are waiting for something better. This excuse—this refusal to see any good in what we have because we compare it to an ideal that does not exist—is our biggest failure. Unless we change this tendency in our thinking, we cannot move forward. What we need, as the European experience teaches, is to seek perfection in the trains we could have right now.

The last time Americans flooded Europe—after World War II—its infrastructure lay in shambles. The United States was the one teaching Europe how to rebuild and to survive. Perhaps we can be forgiven for believing so long afterward that Europe had nothing to teach its saviors. If we saw ourselves as learners, not just as critics, we would open our eyes to the world. We would agree that Europe is now the teacher and that their lesson is on how to make trains happen—luxury trains and commuter trains, conventional and high-speed. We would be willing to look

160

at ourselves from the perspective of Europe's arguments. We would take pride in the American sacrifice that gave Europeans their opportunity and, most important, would see that as our opportunity too.

Simply, Europe would be our classroom. We would enter as often as possible—as citizens, politicians, planners, academics, and engineers—observing the lesson and bringing it home. We would finally agree with Ambassador James Bryce that Europe is our future. We have a growing population and a dwindling land base; we have room to spare but not room to waste. We would agree that transportation should help us preserve the remaining glories of our continent.

In 1999 my wife and I went back to Europe. Although Christine had extensively toured Europe after high school, it had been a guided trip and all by bus. This time we planned to guide ourselves and make up the trip as we went along, and all of it would be on a rail pass. I wanted the opportunity of her fresh, unencumbered perspective on the significance and ease of taking trains. If I were exaggerating the themes of this book, she would tell me; if I were wrong, she would tell me that too.

On the flight to Frankfurt via Copenhagen, we naturally conceded the advantages of airplane speeds—the nonstop flight from Seattle took us directly over the Arctic Circle, so that we were in Copenhagen in just nine and a half hours. Fifty years earlier (and certainly seventy-five) few Americans had the time to make such trips, since crossing the United States by rail required three days and crossing the Atlantic Ocean another seven. Now, even with one transfer, Christine and I would be in Frankfurt in under half a day. Jet travel had certainly made the world smaller and more accessible; relatively speaking, ticket prices were cheaper too. There was no denying the progress the airlines offered for those wishing (or needing) to get somewhere as fast as possible.

However, barely visible beneath us, 5,000 miles of planet earth was silently slipping by. This was the other side of speed—the absence of familiarity. The television monitor alerted us as we bisected Hudson Bay and crossed the edge of northern Greenland. We could not honestly say we had been to either place—instead, the monitor counted off a statistic labeled "miles to destination." We kept wondering aloud about skipping over one-fifth the circumference of the planet. On this trip, explorers we were not.

Frankfurt was how I remembered it from 1982—especially its wealth of public transportation. In the Hauptbahnhof (central railroad station) there was still an abundance of trains arriving and departing. My unexpected find was the new station beside the airport. Previously, the station directly beneath the airport had been for commuters only, and air travelers had used that station, which transferred to the Hauptbahnhof

The *Thunersee* arriving at Interlaken West Station, Switzerland, from Mannheim, Germany, on October 6, 1999, at 5:20 PM. Photograph by the author.

downtown. Now perhaps a third of Frankfurt's major intercity trains came in and out of this new airport station. Arriving passengers simply collected their bags, walked the short distance to the station (with free luggage carts available), and boarded a train without detouring into Frankfurt.

For the moment I stuck with the detour, as we were staying overnight in Frankfurt. At the basement station, we boarded a local train for downtown. We had booked a hotel directly opposite the Hauptbahnhof. Now, with an entire afternoon of daylight still ahead, we decided to dump our luggage, validate our rail pass, and get right into our research. Minutes after registering at the hotel, we returned and headed for the ticket counter. As expected, the agent immediately recognized my American accent and answered me pleasantly in English. "Would you please validate this," I asked, showing him our pass. "Certainly," he replied. "I need only to see your passports."

"Now watch this," I said to Christine. Returning to the concourse, we located the large printed timetables that listed all arriving and departing trains. Departures are printed on yellow sheets, arriving trains on white, all using the European style, the 24-hour clock. "Let's go to Heidelberg," I suggested, "five minutes, track 14." On the platform there was another aid, a train locator, on a board about the size of a movie poster. Found trackside throughout Europe, these train locators show the makeup of every departing train. "See here," I said to Christine. "It shows where each car will be positioned on the platform when the train arrives—first class, the diner, second class, smoking and no-smoking coaches. You find the letter on the platform corresponding with your class of service, then determine where you are supposed to board—A, B, C, and so on. First class for the train to Heidelberg includes positions D and E. A door will open for us within 50 feet." Momentarily, the train arrived and Christine and I were on our way; she was incredulous that it had been so easy even a novice could have figured it out.

Once aboard, we looked for the reservation holders about the size of a business card that indicated a reserved seat. No slip in the holder meant no reservation—just take the seat and settle back. In both first and second class, the traditional arrangement is six-seat compartments, two facing rows of three. Obviously, the window seats get taken first, then the two facing forward—the two backward-facing seats go last. However, since European trains frequently reverse the direction of operation, everyone gets a turn to face forward. In Frankfurt, for example, the majority of tracks dead-end in the station. Departing, even intercity trains reverse direction in order to continue on their way. In 1982 the arriving engine was generally dropped and another was added at the opposite end. However, by 1999, most trains were push-pull combinations; the engine was not dropped but rather set to operate from a cab in the tailing car. An engine that had been pulling the train would suddenly be pushing it, or vice versa.

We found our train practically full. In our compartment, a man in a business suit had the forward-facing window seat. We respected both his leg room and elbow room by sitting opposite him in the two seats by the door. He smiled, so I explained ourselves, noting that we had just landed at the airport not two hours ago. The best cure for jet lag, we had been advised, was not to sleep until nightfall. It had been a good excuse to show Christine how quickly you can board a train in Europe. "Yes," the man replied, speaking better English than my German, "you are the nation of the automobile. You still have all that space."

It was another reminder that Germans, beginning with their artists, have always loved the American West. I recalled that in 1982 the Marlboro

Man had been riding high on signboards along the Rhine (they were not billboards, and none were beside the highway or the tracks). The ad invited Germans to enter a special contest; first prize was a year in the United States, living on a western cattle ranch. The contest had reminded me of Lorelei, the mythical siren of the Rhine whose singing lured boatmen to their deaths. Leave it to Mr. Cancer Stick, I concluded, to pick up where German folklore had left off. Every German puffing his way to an early grave could blame it on the siren song of open space.

I reminded our companion about the growth of American cities. "Yes," he replied soberly, "but at least your dream lives outside them. Bavaria is not the American West."

Arriving in Heidelberg, we left the discussion there and transferred to a local train that would take us back to Mannheim; we waited perhaps ten minutes. In Mannheim, we located our first ICE (intercity express) train, which would whisk us back to Frankfurt. The top speed for these gently futuristic-looking trains is 175 mph. We waited for the ICE barely ten minutes more. Aboard the train, Christine finally succumbed to jet lag and nodded off. I was still too excited to think of sleep. Tomorrow we would follow the Rhine to Düsseldorf, returning to Haan, a picturesque suburb and the birthplace of my father. With his last surviving sister, my Aunt Paula, we would visit the house where he was born. Tomorrow, we could take another ICE train or a dependable intercity; there would be no worries either way. If we missed a train there would be plenty of backup trains, likely no more than fifteen minutes behind—it is that way all over Europe. Between Frankfurt and Düsseldorf alone, an ICE train was scheduled every hour. The other trains, albeit slower, were by no means less comfortable or efficient.

It took only the afternoon for Christine's face to light up with amazement. "You mean it's this easy," she kept repeating. Using three trains in the space of four hours, I too had been totally reassured. Yes, the trains of 1999 were still as good as the trains of 1982—and many were better. Before exiting the station to go to our hotel, we checked the departure board one more time. "Let's take the ICE train tomorrow at 10:46, track nine," I suggested. "There's another at 11:46 if we miss it, but we won't. Either way, we will get a good night's sleep."

The following week spent touring the Rhine was a lesson in wonder and efficiency. We rode trains every day, and everywhere in the valley, taking advantage of the approximately thirty passenger trains *per hour* that follow the river's path. In addition to the locals, the ICE trains, and intercities, whole sets of new commuter trains had been added to serve Mainz, Koblenz, and Cologne. These were available on our rail pass too; rarely did we wait longer than ten minutes for any train, regardless of the time or destination. Better yet, the Eurail Pass is interchangeable with most of the river cruise lines. All ships stop to disembark and board passengers convenient to the railroad stations. You simply get a ticket (free with the pass) and hop aboard.

The Rhine has been a major transportation corridor, for Germany and for all of Europe, for two thousand years. The valley's population density and the ease of transport explain the frequency of its trains. Immediately to the north of Germany lies Holland, so the Rhine is also the major north–south corridor between northern Europe and Italy, with Switzerland in between.

Europe is careful not to let any route fall below a reasonable number of trains. Even a train whose primary focus is one of the major corridors will often end the day splitting off from it. Trains traveling north and south along the Rhine will leave the corridor before repeating the trip, perhaps heading east to Berlin or west to Paris—or at least some of their cars will make it there. European trains split and reassemble in minutes, again with the idea of leaving no one out.

Of course, major cities get the most trains; linking the largest concentrations of population with the most frequent trains is only common sense. It is what happens next that makes the difference: Europe does not stop with the largest cities, as if the smaller ones do not exist. Europe's philosophy (contrasting with America's parochialism) is that every community deserves rail passenger service. In Europe, there would be no way that cities like Boston, New York, and Philadelphia would get half the trains in the country and cities like Binghamton not even one.

Europe knows that if the traveler on a main line cannot connect to the smaller cities within a couple of hours, the incentive for using public transportation is proportionally reduced in the big cities too. The state knows better than to tell people where they can or should want to go. In the United States, if Christine and I were in Washington DC and wished to go to Binghamton, we could get only as far as New York—still 175 miles away. We might as well just rent a car in Washington and drive straight to Binghamton in the first place.

Since there is no train to Binghamton, it is a decision I have regrettably made many times, which means I did not travel the Northeast Corridor at all—revenue that Amtrak might have had but never saw. Now that we were in Europe, there would be no such missing links. Instead, we might contribute to the strength of corridors by being enticed to use their connections. Whatever our preference, it would be served. Where was it that *we* wished to go? Europe is not about narrowing those opportunities; need is apportioned but not denied. Europe is about networking

travel, not building lines. Gathering passengers from around the network increases the number of passengers on every corridor too.

Restoring trains in the United States depends on adopting the same perspective that trains should serve people where they actually live—that is the meaning of networking. Don't tell me I should move—a citizen in Binghamton is as much a citizen as anyone living in New York City. This goes back to Amtrak's (and the railroads') inherent, historical failure. Few in Congress ever intended Amtrak to be responsible outside of a few major markets. Rather, people in the United States were supposed to act absurdly—as long as a train was "close," passengers should be willing to reach it.

As much as I have put up with the inconvenience of modern train travel for the love of research, who in their right mind expects that of anyone? The time and expense of getting to the train do matter; no one would do that regularly. Europe knows better than to provide absurd travel opportunities and then blame people for never using them.

A reasonable schedule begins with a reasonable minimum of trains: at least one in the morning, afternoon, and night. In Europe, the minimum is several per hour; in the United States, it is no less important that every station be served by at least one train at the most convenient time. Historically, both sections of the *Phoebe Snow* departed Binghamton between 2:00 and 3:00 PM, putting her in Elmira, New York, between 1:00 and 4:00 in the afternoon, and in Scranton, Pennsylvania, between 2:00 and 3:00 (the directions there merely reversed). Regionally, three population centers totaling 400,000 people got the best train on the Lackawanna Railroad in the middle of the day. Additional evening trains and morning trains satisfied other markets and other needs.

Observing the trains of Europe anywhere, one senses immediately that commitment to efficiency. Scheduling is realistic—to say nothing of frequent—and the infrastructure is fully modernized. There is double track practically everywhere, even on both sides of the Rhine. Four tracks mean no interference between freight and passenger services. For that matter, freight trains are much lighter (and considerably shorter) than in the United States. Generally, freight trains tend to travel on the east side of the river, interspersed with local and regional passenger trains.

Lauterbrunnen Valley, Switzerland's Yosemite, is not wilderness, but it is certainly beautiful and completely accessible by train (1982). Photograph by the author.

The west bank is reserved entirely for passengers—and the fastest trains—during the busiest times of the day.

Still, and just as important, the Rhine has not lost its charm. Although the river is one of the busiest routes in Europe, it remains among the most scenic and historic. That is especially true along the lower Rhine, renowned for its castle-studded bluffs, and vineyards climbing high into the hills. Germany considers this a magical landscape and asks that its railroads behave accordingly. The coexistence of commerce and tourism demands that the railroad be a preservationist and more, that the railroad be preserved. Adding a major highway would ruin everything, as would straightening the tracks to allow greater speeds. Cuts and fills on the railroad have been held to a minimum and where exposed, were made to look like medieval walls. Tunnel portals resembling castle towers complement the actual ruins high above. It is a reminder of the historical relationship between rivers and railroads in the United States, a charm and stewardship, as we have seen, that faded rapidly with the spread of highways.

In Europe, wherever the scenery and the history call for stewardship, even the fastest trains accept slowing down. Progress is not just going fast; rather, it is a commitment to efficiency across the board. In the United States, even trains on main-line tracks experience a precipitous drop in efficiency when departing a station. Thumping and bumping their way past yards and sidings, passenger trains take forever getting back up to speed; arriving trains have the same problem. Europe knows better than to believe that the difference can be made up between stations. In Europe, the object is also consistency, entering and departing every station swiftly, without which sustaining movement in the middle of a trip is meaningless. European railroads know that to maintain a good speed, they must do more than achieve temporary high speeds. Efficiency requires smooth and seamless service at every point in the trip.

Now enthralled, Christine and I next planned a week of research in the Alps, visiting railroads instructive of preserving scenery. Because our obvious choice was Switzerland, I reread an article by Eric Julber, a Los Angeles attorney who had stirred up a hornet's nest in the 1970s with his suggestion in *Reader's Digest* that trains and cable cars should be allowed in Yosemite Valley. Why not perch a restaurant on top of Half Dome; why not a glass of wine with your evening meal? Europeans were doing it everywhere. The American wilderness should be like Switzerland, more accessible if not more civilized. Only elitists maintained that visitors too frail to hike should not be allowed trains and trams.[1]

To say the least, most environmentalists at the time, including me, had been incensed. Trains *inside* the national parks? Finally, in 1982, I had escaped the gulf of cultures and spent a month following in Julber's footsteps. Exploring the Alps by rail, I found reason to be receptive. In the United States, the biggest scars on the landscape always seemed to be the result of building highways. Americans had built roads through the national parks, so why get upset about building trams? At least we should admit that roads in the parks are invasive too.

Ignoring a cable car to Glacier Point (which I still oppose), what about Yosemite Valley? One square mile out of its precious seven had already been developed, much of it under asphalt. A railroad into the valley proper could hardly be more damaging than the highway—it was the highway that fed the parking lots. Eric Julber was closer to the facts than I wished to admit. In no park would the general public tolerate being excluded just to appease environmentalists; however, the public might accept excluding cars if convinced of the necessity. Democracy demanded that the public be given a fair alternative. As in Switzerland, a tastefully designed railroad running on a convenient schedule might be that alternative—both access and preservation would be served.[2] Instead of the 30-foot road and shoulders, the railroad could be just several feet across; its capacity would still be significantly greater than the existing highway.

Switzerland indeed offers a grand comparison: the glorious Lauterbrunnen Valley in the Bernese Alps. Eager to assess Christine's reaction, I had planned we would wind up there. Generally, the weather in northern Germany foretells the weather in the Alps. Along the Rhine, it had been raining off and on the entire week. Fortunately, that had not spoiled our stay in the least. By late morning the clouds had lifted to reveal the castles and hills. After visiting my aunt, we went to St. Goar to explore the nearby towns. Finally, the sky showed evidence of clearing and we agreed: it was time for Switzerland!

We checked out of the hotel at 10:00 AM, and walked one block to St. Goar station, where we boarded the first train south. It turned out to be a commuter that would take us as far as Mainz; there we dashed across the platform and transferred to the intercity *Tiziano*. Approaching Mannheim an hour later, I noticed on the timetable that we had another choice: we could either remain aboard the *Tiziano* or transfer to the ICE *Thunersee*. Without further transfer, the *Thunersee* would take us to Interlaken, the gateway to the Bernese Alps. Better yet, we would arrive two hours sooner, preserving daylight all the way. I sprang to my feet and grabbed our suitcases, announcing to Christine our change of plans.

Ten minutes later we had boarded the *Thunersee*, Christine still laughing about our getaway. It seemed I would do anything to prove that trains in Europe are frequent and easy. "Okay, professor, but you owe me lunch," Christine said, pushing me suggestively towards the dining car.

The sky now a brilliant blue, I promised that after lunch we would see the Alps rising on the approach to Bern.

My first sight of the Alps in 1982 had taken my breath away. Seeing them again, towering above those emerald valleys, I wondered why I had waited so long to return. But finally we were there. Now Christine was getting educated, learning how the ease of our arrival intertwined with stewardship. We were on only one of a hundred trains speeding toward the mountains, following perhaps a dozen different routes. Earlier that morning or the previous day, those trains had been in Amsterdam, Madrid, Rome, Frankfurt, Paris, and Milan. For all those people and all those visitors, the decision not to bring a car had been a simple one. With so many railroads feeding into Switzerland, and the Swiss themselves providing dozens more for travel within the country, who would think of seeing the countryside any other way?

The *Thunersee* was soon living up to its namesake, paralleling the majestic lake as it approached Interlaken from the west. Back in Germany and north of Bern, we had averaged 125 mph. Now that we were entering a scenic district, the train cut its speed in half; it was time for slowing down, for savoring all we had come to see. Never should the practical overwhelm the spiritual. Upholding the spirit of preservation, at times we slowed even more, as the train followed curves gently molded into the hillsides or along the shore. Time and again the mountains opened, then closed again, the lake always a brilliant blue to our left. Then the conductor was announcing our arrival—after a passage as memorable as any on the face of Europe, we disembarked at Interlaken West station just minutes past 5:00 PM.

Once more, the discrepancy between trains in Europe and the United States came sharply into focus. Nothing in America recalled railroading so beautiful and so convenient—not in Flagstaff, Arizona; Glenwood Springs, Colorado; or even Glacier National Park. I imagined trains as beautiful as the *Thunersee* arriving daily at the Grand Canyon—perhaps with dozens of trains originating in Los Angeles. We had just come an equivalent distance, approximately 450 miles; with two transfers, we still averaged 70 mph. Nothing as imposing as the Alps would have slowed our train across the Mojave Desert. Why not consider that future for the Grand Canyon before planning huge parking lots on the boundary? There could be trains from Phoenix and Chicago too.

The whole of Switzerland is barely the size of a smaller American state; however, Americans often use that argument selfishly, as if only America has land to waste. The continental United States may have double the space of western Europe (adding in the British Isles), but that is not to say it has twice the usable space. Our wasteful history and wasteful

Beside Lake Brienz, Switzerland's *Panorama Express* has just departed Interlaken East Station, bound for Lucerne, October 9, 1999. Note the tremendous windows. Photograph by the author.

habits continue to keep the United States from appreciating how much like Europe it has become.

The following morning, departing Interlaken for Lauterbrunnen Valley, Christine and I picked up on those themes again. Like most visitors, we boarded the narrow-gauge, cog-assisted railroad for our climb into the mountains. At Lauterbrunnen, we transferred for the steepest leg to Wengen and Kleine Scheidig. The next day we returned, taking the funicular up the valley's eastern side; atop the cliffs, another narrow-gauge railroad leads to Mürren, where a breathtaking hike to the picturesque town of Gimmelwald begins. "This place is for real," noted our guidebook, part of Switzerland's authentic "cowbell country."[3]

Getting to Gimmelwald was the easy part: an hour walk, but all downhill. In the village, hikers are tempted by another cable car—no need to even think of struggling back. In minutes you can drop again to the valley floor. We were tempted, but our recent encounters with afternoon coffee and pastries dictated we get the exercise. After huffing and puffing through our return to Mürren, we rewarded ourselves at the first bakery we spotted, the one closest to the trail.

It was not wilderness, not even close. We still agreed with the American model; we would not want for our national parks and public lands to have the same intensity of development. Lauterbrunnen is spoken for on every slope; where no farm or village commands the landscape, there is likely a ski run or hotel. Even the steepest hillsides are hayed and grazed. On the other hand, the high country is spectacular, the automobile is gloriously absent, and the valley has only narrow roads. What traffic there is makes little noise. The least we might do for America's national parks is copy Switzerland's technical elegance. By using rail in the parks' most visited portions, we might make a better threshold for landscape and wilderness both.

As the oft-touted geological counterpart of Yosemite Valley, Lauterbrunnen makes that point. Each places owes its grandeur to resilient granite and the sculpting of mighty glaciers. The cliffs of both are alive with greenery and the majesty of hanging waterfalls. All visitors deserve to see these things—it is how they see them where these two differ. Switzerland's enviable control over the car makes the Lauterbrunnen landscape appear spacious even with the crowds. It is not wilderness that the visitor sees, but Lauterbrunnen is definitely worth seeing, and more than once.

Switzerland's countryside is the progressives' dream—everything is beautiful, not only the parks. Lauterbrunnen has country lanes, not highways, and few Americans would even call them roads. Though not total wilderness, Switzerland still maintains the middle ground. I felt the return of all the good feelings I had lost at places like Wyalusing and Gaviota; I felt reassurance that any landscape could be developed without being destroyed.

In Switzerland, the trade-off for protected wilderness is a private landscape served by the stewardship of public trains. The object is not that the government always owns the landscape, but rather that its beauty owns peoples' hearts.

It hardly matters what the system is with that kind of commitment. The railroad into Lauterbrunnen is privately owned, and the major lines remain primarily nationalized. We found the private railroads and the government railroads working side by side—and saw it again on the *Panorama Express* to Lucerne and the narrow-gauge to Gstaad. Climbing everywhere into the mountains, we were little aware of who owned the trains. Clearly, the most important system in Switzerland is the system of cooperation. The country is all about protecting values.

Christine and I discussed stewardship further on the return to Frankfurt, now riding the *Berner Oberland*. Too often, the United States looks first for a magic formula, as if the system is the value. Should it not be the other way around? Should we not first identify the values we want preserved and *then* build the system? That is what the railroads of Europe do. Europe is beyond America's excuse that the debate should begin with labels instead of values. Allowing trains to inspire and serve us in the United States means getting back to those values too. There is no perfect system and no magic formula; rather, it begins with a change of heart. If we believe that the wonder of distance is the American dream—a dream we just might miss—we would be wise to start thinking like Europe.

The Land Would Ask for Trains

In a famous picture by the logging photographer Darius Kinsey, a pioneer family has carved a clearing from old-growth forest in Washington State. Great trees have been felled and cut into lengths, their stumps 5 and 6 feet across. A cabin, fence, and outhouse confirm a picture of human toil. This photograph is a telling reminder of why Americans have resisted preservation. For Americans, not until wilderness became the opposite of daily life could it be loved and understood. "Appreciation of wilderness began in cities," notes the historian Roderick Frazier Nash. "The literary gentleman wielding a pen, not the pioneer with his axe, made the first gestures of resistance against the strong currents of antipathy."[1]

Although the railroads were a principal cause of changing wilderness, they hardly wanted the dishevelment of the pioneers. The railroads asked the same literary Americans who defended wilderness to write for them, and commissioned hundreds of artists to paint pictures, confirming their respect for emerging landscapes. These places were not wilderness, but they could be beautiful. Since that time, nothing has taken the place of the railroads in their ability to keep the magic of exploration alive. Today, America is traveling blind.

To restore the railroads' respect for natural beauty hardly requires a leap of faith. They are a technology we have known and used. And even if we ignored the history, they remain the perfect investment in ourselves.

Arriving Binghamton, New York, the westbound *Phoebe Snow* pauses for passengers in January 1965. Despite a frozen passage from New York City, the train has arrived on time. Normally, poor weather closes the highway and airport. All across America, the loss of passenger trains cost communities choice and the best friend landscape ever had. Photograph courtesy of Walter E. Smith.

These would be American trains, built and run by American workers—thousands of good jobs for years to come.

There again, we should not need to keep proving what works. History confirms that the proper level of trains is a minimum of three a day. Every American city with a population over 50,000 deserves a train in the morning, afternoon, and night; every one of those routes deserves a double track. By starting with a system that is convenient and usable, its proper growth would take care of itself.

In Europe, the key to success is sincerity. In the United States, our lack of sincerity is demonstrated by an absurd insistence that single trains can do the job. Invariably, when trains fail, critics blame the technology, as if anyone allowed on a highway only once every twenty-four hours would blame the car and call it inconvenient. Adding to the problem is bulk and weight: in Europe, freight trains tend to be light and short; in the United States, most are heavy and long. In Europe, a freight train can slip onto an adjacent track, be passed, and just as rapidly resume full speed. In the United States, railroads complain incessantly about passenger trains when it is the freight trains that move too slowly.

Just building new rights-of-way dedicated to high-speed trains will never solve the problem. The problem is our lack of confidence—we no longer trust railroads or know them well enough to disagree. They insist that the problem is capacity but won't admit how they lost it. The railroads would like us to believe that their operations are mystical, especially the economics. Decades ago, when they ran 20,000 passenger trains, the railroads never complained about capacity; they provided the needed tracks. Europe has always provided them. If American railroads keep losing to their competitors, it will be a problem they brought on themselves.[2]

But all these problems could be solved. Only the obstructionist asks for the particulars, then says no to every one. These days, too many critics prefer being obstructionists. At the very least, a switch from private railroads to an interstate railroad network would open the tracks to everyone. By definition, highways and airports are already nationalized—constructed, operated, and owned by the government. Air traffic control is a federal responsibility. Why should government play with labels? Whose feelings might we possibly hurt?

Aldo Leopold's words provide an eloquent call to action: "Examine each question in terms of what is ethically and aesthetically right, as well as what is economically expedient. A thing is right when it tends to preserve the integrity, stability, and beauty of the biotic community. It is wrong when it tends otherwise."[3] Adds Georgie Anne Geyer, "There are those, no doubt about it, who will answer with figures. Trains are not practical any more, trains are not financially feasible, trains are not...*I don't care*...I am talking now about something else; I am saying that I, for one, am tired of living in microcosms connected by Flight 234."[4]

We should remember that trains were an invention that turned out right for life and for landscape. And so, in the twenty-first century, railroads remain travel's integrity and stability. Finally, it is time our technical prowess agreed with our hearts. There is no technology worth sacrificing the nation we have pledged to be. The land would ask for trains. For the good of America the United, and America the Beautiful, we need to believe in the land again, and go by train.

Notes

Prologue: The Earth on Display

1. Western Pacific Railway; Denver & Rio Grande Railroad; Missouri Pacific Railway; and St. Louis, Iron Mountain & Southern Railway, *The Globe at the San Francisco Exposition,* Souvenir Pamphlet, 1915.
2. Atchison, Topeka & Santa Fe Railway, "Grand Canyon at the Panama-Pacific International Exposition, San Francisco," in *Coast Lines Time Tables, Corrected to 1915* (Chicago: Atchison, Topeka & Santa Fe Railway, 1915); and Union Pacific System, "Yellowstone National Park: Exhibit of Union Pacific System at Panama-Pacific International Exposition," in *California and the Expositions* (Omaha: Union Pacific System, 1915), 12–16. The enormity and significance of the exposition is beautifully detailed in Robert A. Reid, *The Blue Book: A Comprehensive Official Souvenir View Book of the Panama-Pacific International Exposition at San Francisco, 1915* (San Francisco: Panama-Pacific International Exposition Co., 1915).
3. Reid, *The Blue Book,* 100, 311–26; and Great Northern Railway, "Great Northern Railway Exhibit Building, Panama-Pacific International Exposition, San Francisco, California," Promotional Postcard, 1915.
4. U.S. Department of the Interior, *Proceedings of the National Park Conference Held at Berkeley, California, March 11, 12, and 13, 1915* (Washington DC: Government Printing Office, 1915).
5. Western Pacific et al., *The Globe.*

1 — The Places We Rode

1. Peter Lyon, *To Hell in a Day Coach: An Exasperated Look at American Railroads* (Philadelphia: J. B. Lippincott, 1968), 227.
2. Georgie Anne Geyer, "Here, the Pieces of Life Flow Together," *Los Angeles Times,* July 22, 1977, section CC, part II.
3. Of course, the railroads forfeited much of this territory, reducing their total from 180 million to 129 million acres. See Roy M. Robbins, *Our Landed Heritage: The Public Domain, 1776–1936* (Lincoln: University of Nebraska Press, 1962), 223–25.
4. Clive Irving, "If You Think This Is Travel, You're Crazy," *Condé Nast Traveler,* September 1992, 129.
5. Irving, "If You Think This Is Travel," 129.
6. Susan Danly and Leo Marx, eds., *The Railroad in American Art: Representations of Technological Change* (Cambridge, MA: MIT Press, 1988), 5–7. See also Barbara Novak, "Man's Traces: Axe, Train, and Figure," in *Nature and Culture: American Landscape and Painting, 1825–1875* (New York: Oxford University Press, 1980), 157–200, esp. 175.
7. A fascinating history of a railroad commission is Nicolai Cikovsky Jr., "George Inness's *The Lackawanna Valley*: 'Type of the Modern,'" in *The Railroad in American Art,* ed. Danly and Marx, 71–91.

8. The railroad origins of the national parks are summarized in Alfred Runte, *Trains of Discovery: Western Railroads and the National Parks*, 4th ed. (Boulder, CO: Roberts Rinehart, 1998).

9. Robin W. Winks, *Frederick Billings: A Life* (New York: Oxford University Press, 1991), 285. Of course, the hope was not without contradictions, and Billings had by no means advocated a pristine landscape.

10. *North by Northwest*, directed by Alfred Hitchcock, performances by Cary Grant, Eva Marie Saint, James Mason, Martin Landau, et al., Metro-Goldwyn-Mayer, 1959. Another wonderful motion picture depicting the allure of trains is *Before Sunrise*, directed by Richard Linklater, performances by Ethan Hawke, Julie Delpy, et al., Castle Rock, 1995.

11. A recent history of the train is Karl R. Zimmerman, *20th Century Limited* (St. Paul, MN: Motorbooks International, 2002).

2 — The Legacy of Phoebe Snow

1. "Census Bureau Projects Doubling of Nation's Population by 2100," *U.S. Census Bureau News* (January 13, 2000). Current statistics may be followed in U.S. Bureau of the Census, *Statistical Abstract of the United States,* published annually (Washington DC: Government Printing Office). Refer to section 1, Population.

2. U.S. Bureau of the Census, *Statistical Abstract: 2004–2005*, 214.

3. For a detailed history of the Lackawanna Railroad, see Thomas Townsend Taber, *The Delaware, Lackawanna & Western Railroad: The Road of Anthracite in the Nineteenth Century, 1828–1899* (Muncy, PA: T. T. Taber, 1977).

4. An important new history of the African American experience on the railroads is Larry Tye, *Rising from the Rails: Pullman Porters and the Making of the Black Middle Class* (New York: Henry Holt, 2004).

5. The process is beautifully described in Peter T. Maiken, *Night Trains: The Pullman System in the Golden Years of American Rail Travel* (Chicago: Lakme Press, 1989). For a state-by-state listing, see 313–405.

6. Delaware, Lackawanna & Western Railroad, "New Passenger Station of the Lackawanna at Scranton, Pennsylvania," Press Release, November 11, 1908 (reproduction in the files of Lackawanna Station Hotel). An important history of the station, including full descriptions and photographs of the panels, is U.S. Department of the Interior, National Park Service, Steamtown National Historic Site, *Lackawanna Station: Scranton, Pennsylvania,* by Paul Trap, October 31, 1996.

3 — What Europe Is Teaching Still

1. Two recent assessments are Jane Holtz Kay, *Asphalt Nation: How the Automobile Took Over America, and How We Can Take It Back* (New York: Crown, 1997); and Clay McShane, *Down the Asphalt Path: The Automobile and the American City* (New York: Columbia University Press, 1994).

2. Aldo Leopold, *A Sand County Almanac* (New York: Oxford University Press, 1968), 210.

4 — Dismemberment and Farewell

1. Tom Cawley, "Phoebe Snow Finally Jilted: ICC Orders 4 Trains Dropped," *The Evening Press* (Binghamton, NY), November 10, 1966, 1–B; and Cawley, "The Old Glory of Railroading is Fading Fast," *The Sunday Press* (Binghamton, NY), November 13, 1966, 1–C.

2. Frederick Law Olmsted, *Civilizing American Cities: A Selection of Frederick Law Olmsted's Writings on City Landscapes*, ed. S. B. Sutton (Cambridge, MA: MIT Press, 1971); and William H. Whyte, *The Last Landscape* (Garden City, NY: Doubleday, 1968).

3. Claiborne Pell, *Megalopolis Unbound: The Supercity and the Transportation of Tomorrow* (New York: Praeger, 1966).
4. Lyon, *To Hell in a Day Coach*, esp. 223–55.
5. See Lyon, *To Hell in a Day Coach*, 180. Young is most famous for this advertising quote: "A hog can cross the country without changing trains—but you can't."

5 — Vows Made to Rivers

1. In the distinguished Rivers of America Series, the classic history is Carl Carmer, *The Susquehanna* (New York: Rinehart, 1955).
2. The web site of the Federal Highway Administration, U.S. Department of Transportation, still makes reference to these awards. See "FHWA By Day: A Look at the History of the Federal Highway Administration," http://www.fhwa.dot.gov/byday/fhbd0830.htm (accessed January 10, 2005). A biography of Lady Bird Johnson's environmental activism, with much on billboards, is Lewis L. Gould, *Lady Bird Johnson and the Environment* (Lawrence: University Press of Kansas, 1988).
3. The classic example is *Starrucca Viaduct, Pennsylvania* (1865) by Jasper Francis Cropsey. For a full-color reproduction, see Danly and Marx, eds., *The Railroad in American Art*, 12.
4. See again Novak, "Man's Traces," 157–200.
5. Oliver Jensen, "A Cautionary Tale," *American Heritage* 20 (December 1968): 10–15.
6. Jensen, "A Cautionary Tale," 13.
7. In perhaps the best one-volume history of the environmental movement, railroads are mentioned only once, and then in reference to the conversion of railroad rights-of-way into recreational trails. See Samuel P. Hays, *Beauty, Health, and Permanence: Environmental Politics in the United States, 1955–1985* (Cambridge: Cambridge University Press, 1987), 290.
8. Under the Wild and Scenic Rivers Act, rivers paralleled by railroads could at best be considered "recreational," giving those waterways the lowest level of protection. Ironically, a river could still be classified as "scenic" (giving it a higher level of protection) if "accessible in places by road," but not if accessible by railroad. U.S. Department of the Interior, National Park Service; and U.S. Department of Agriculture, U.S. Forest Service, *Guidelines for Evaluating Wild, Scenic, and Recreational River Areas Proposed for Inclusion in the National Wild and Scenic Rivers System Under Section 2, Public Law 90–542*, February 1970.
9. As a board member of the Susquehanna Conservation Council, I initially wrote against the Army Corps of Engineers' proposals in Binghamton's morning newspaper; Alfred Runte, "The Susquehanna: Use with Care," *The Sun-Bulletin*, March 12, 1971, 1, 6–7. My last critique was "Shining River: The Susquehanna," *The Conservationist* (New York) 30 (March–April 1976): 14–18. After extensive public hearings in 1976, the corps withdrew its report.
10. Henry David Thoreau, *Walden* (New York: New American Library, 1942), 129.

6 — The Debate We Never Had

1. U.S. Department of Transportation, Federal Railroad Administration, *High-Speed Ground Transportation for America* (September 1997), chap. 1; and Lyon, *To Hell in a Day Coach*, 268–73.
2. U.S. Bureau of the Census, *Statistical Abstract, 1976*, 67. In 1972, automobile fatalities reached an all-time high of 56,278, for an annual death rate of 27 people per 100,000 of population.

3. Lyon, *To Hell in a Day Coach,* 126. A lively account of railroad accidents may be found in Oliver Jensen, *The American Heritage History of Railroads in America* (New York: American Heritage, 1975), 178–89.

4. In 2002, a total of 42,815 Americans died in motor vehicle accidents. U.S. Bureau of the Census, *Statistical Abstract, 2004–2005,* 698.

5. National Safety Council, "What Are the Odds of Dying?" March 2004, http://www.nsc.org/lrs/statinfo/odds.htm (accessed January 20, 2005); and Kopl Halperin, "A Comparative Analysis of Six Methods for Calculating Travel Fatality Risk," *Risk: Health, Safety & Environment* 4 (1993): 15.

6. U.S. Department of the Interior, National Park Service, Park Net, "Casualties at Antietam" (table of American deaths in all wars), http://www.nps.gov/anti/casualty.htm (accessed January 20, 2005).

7. Lyon, *To Hell in a Day Coach,* 249–54.

8. See Karl R. Zimmermann, *CZ: The Story of the* California Zephyr (Starrucca, PA: Starrucca Valley Publications, 1972).

9. A period introduction to these trains at the beginning of the Amtrak era is Patrick C. Dorin, *The Domeliners: A Pictorial History of the Penthouse Trains* (Seattle: Superior Publishing, 1973).

7 — The Quick Fix

1. Tom Cawley, "Phoebe Snow Finally Jilted."

2. A seminal, period article on the problem of railroad economics is Stanley Berge, "Why Kill the Passenger Train?" *Journal of Marketing* 28 (January 1964): 1–6.

3. The classic case is the merger of the Pennsylvania and New York Central Railroads in 1968. See Joseph R. Daughen and Peter Binzen, *The Wreck of the Penn Central* (Boston: Little, Brown, 1971). On the handsome value of the Erie-Lackawanna after liquidation, see H. Roger Grant, *Erie Lackawanna: Death of an American Railroad, 1938–1992* (Palo Alto, CA: Stanford University Press, 1994), 210–28.

4. On September 30, 1965, having just signed the High-Speed Ground Transportation Act, President Lyndon B. Johnson met privately with railroad executives at the White House. It was reported that the president asked them to reconsider dropping so many trains. If so, they obviously ignored him. See Lyon, *To Hell in a Day Coach,* 258–59.

5. There are no comprehensive histories of Amtrak. Meanwhile, a welcome departure from the standard fare of rail-fan histories is Gordon Gill, *Amtrak's Long-Distance Service: Can It Be Made Viable?* (Pittsburgh: Dorrance, 1998); for Amtrak's beginnings, see 1–52. See also Mike Schafer, *All Aboard Amtrak* (Piscataway, NJ: Railpace, 1991), 8–9.

6. Gill, *Amtrak's Long-Distance Service,* 34.

7. A period criticism of Amtrak's arrogance toward its customers is Rush Loving Jr., "Amtrak Is About to Miss the Train," *Fortune* 89 (May 1974): 272–90.

8. Period articles supporting my interpretation are numerous. See, for example, "People Crowd Trains Again, Find Problems—and Pleasures," *U.S. News & World Report,* July 2, 1973, 59–61; and "Train Travel Is Worth Another Try," *Changing Times: The Kiplinger Magazine,* May 1978, 45–47. As early as 1972, the Harris Poll reported national figures indicating that 66 percent of Americans, versus 12 percent against, felt that "it was worth federal subsidies to continue to make intercity train travel available." Support included a 53 percent majority, versus 30 percent against, "believing that the federal government had a responsibility to improve long-distance trains." Louis Harris and Associates Inc., *The Continuing Public Mandate To Improve Inter-City Rail Passenger Travel: Final Report Conducted for Amtrak, the National Railroad Passenger Corporation,* Poll Report, March 1978, 1.

9. Gill, *Amtrak's Long-Distance Service,* 30–36; and Schafer, *All Aboard Amtrak,* 8–9.

10. I am indebted for my statistics to several period sources, including the late Charles Luna, a member of the Amtrak board, and Arthur L. Lloyd, Amtrak Director of Public Affairs, Western Region.

11. For an early criticism of Amtrak's new equipment designs, see Alfred Runte, "In Defense of Passenger Train Aesthetics," *Passenger Train Journal* 9 (April 1977): 20–23.

12. A harsh criticism of the incentive program is U.S. Comptroller General, General Accounting Office, *Amtrak's Incentive Contracts with Railroads: Considerable Cost, Few Benefits. National Railroad Passenger Corporation: Report to the Congress* (Washington DC: General Accounting Office, 1977).

8 Tunnel Vision

1. Paul Seidenman, "Reistrup at the Throttle: Amtrak Picking Up Steam," *Federal Times,* March 7, 1977.

2. National Railroad Passenger Corporation, Office of Public Affairs, *Amtrak Ridership by Route, October–December 1992 vs. October–December 1993.* Monthly Release(s). (Washington DC: National Railroad Passenger Corporation, 1993).

3. Amtrak's commuter operations are described (and criticized) in Joseph Vranich, *Derailed: What Went Wrong and What to Do About America's Passenger Trains* (New York: St. Martin's, 1997), 111–14.

4. U.S. Department of Transportation, Bureau of Transportation Statistics, National Travel Household Survey, "Long Distance Travel Quick Facts," (2002). For purposes of the survey, long distance was defined as greater than 50 miles, resulting in 56 percent of trips for pleasure (vacations, sightseeing, visiting friends and relatives, or outdoor recreation); 16 percent for business; and 13 percent for commuting to work. See also Travel Industry Association of America, "Travel Statistics & Trends," http://www.tia.org/Travel/traveltrends.asp (accessed January 21, 2005).

5. National Railroad Passenger Corporation, *Annual Report 1976* (Washington DC: National Railroad Passenger Corporation, 1976), 8.

6. Alfred Runte, "Long-Distance Trains: Potential for Profit," *Washington Post,* March 19, 1979, A–23.

7. On the problems of improving the Corridor, see U.S. Comptroller General, General Accounting Office, *Problems in the Northeast Railway Improvement Project* (Washington DC: General Accounting Office, 1979).

8. National Railroad Passenger Corporation, *Annual Report 1989* (Washington DC: National Railroad Passenger Corporation, 1989), inside front cover. Categories listed include Revenues (millions); Expenses (millions); Revenue-to-Short-Term Avoidable Cost Ratio; Revenue-to-Long-Term Avoidable Cost Ratio; Passenger Miles (millions); Passenger Miles Per Train-Mile; Ridership (millions) System; Contract Commuter; and Systemwide On-Time Performance. Page 21 divides Amtrak ridership into the familiar categories (Northeast Corridor, Short Distance, and Long Distance), but lumps passenger miles together. It is also interesting to note that while the Northeast Corridor had stayed virtually flat for fourteen years, long-distance ridership in 1989 was up to 5.5 million from 4.5 million in 1976.

9. Stanley Berge, "Why Kill the Passenger Train?" 1–2.

9 — Home Again, and Santa Barbara

1. The periodical literature of the Progressive Era constantly addressed these themes. See, for example, J. Horace McFarland, "Shall We Have Ugly Conservation?" *The Outlook* 91 (March 13, 1909): 594–98; and Allen Chamberlain, "Scenery as a National Asset," *The Outlook* 95 (May 28, 1910): 157–69.

2. McFarland, "Shall We Have Ugly Conservation?" 594.

3. An engaging history of a city and its hinterlands is William Cronon, *Nature's Metropolis: Chicago and the Great West* (New York: W. W. Norton, 1991).

4. J. Horace McFarland, "Why Billboard Advertising as At Present Conducted is Doomed," *Chautauquan* 51 (June 1908): 20, 32.

5. Arthur Reed Kimble, "A Chance for Scenery," *The Outlook* 60 (November 26, 1898): 773–74.

6. Kimble, "A Chance for Scenery," 773–74.

7. A brief history is Alfred Runte, "Promoting the Golden West: Advertising and the Railroad." *California History* 70 (Spring 1991): 62–75.

8. Robert Louis Stevenson, *Across the Plains: With Other Memories and Essays* (New York: Charles Scribner's Sons, 1892), 11.

10 — Gateway to Wilderness

1. The two most relevant are "Pragmatic Alliance: Western Railroads and the National Parks," *National Parks and Conservation Magazine: The Environmental Journal* 48 (April 1974): 14–21; and "Yosemite Valley Railroad: Highway of History, Pathway of Promise," *National Parks and Conservation Magazine: The Environmental Journal* 48 (December 1974): 4–9.

2. Ernest Callenbach, *Ecotopia: The Notebooks and Reports of William Weston* (Berkeley, CA: Banyan Tree Books, 1975).

11 — Designing for Nature

1. Edward Abbey, *Desert Solitaire: A Season in the Wilderness* (New York: Ballantine, 1968), 60.

2. Abbey, *Desert Solitaire*, 246.

3. Leopold, *A Sand County Almanac*, 176–77.

4. Mary Roberts Rinehart, "The Sleeping Giant," *Ladies' Home Journal* 38 (May 1921): 20. Although this article referred to parks in general, her inspiration, from 1915, remained Glacier's park hotels. See "Through Glacier National Park with Howard Eaton," Parts 1 and 2. *Collier's* 57 (April 22, 1916): 11–13, 34–36; 58 (April 29, 1916): 20–21, 26–28.

5. These tragedies are recounted in Jack Olsen, *Night of the Grizzlies* (New York: Putnam, 1969).

6. A scholarly account of tourist deaths in one park is Lee H. Whittlesey, *Death in Yellowstone: Accidents and Foolhardiness in the First National Park* (Boulder, CO: Roberts Rinehart, 1995).

7. Two recent histories of park design are Linda Flint McClelland, *Building the National Parks: The Historic Landscape Design of the National Park Service* (Baltimore: Johns Hopkins University Press, 1998); and Ethan Carr, *Wilderness by Design: Landscape Architecture and the National Park Service* (Lincoln: University of Nebraska Press, 1999).

8. The history of park lodges is the subject of a recent series on public television (PBS). The companion book to the series is Christine Barnes, *Great Lodges of the National Parks* (Bend, OR: W. W. West, 2002).

12 — Grand Canyon

1. As quoted in Roderick Frazier Nash, *Wilderness and the American Mind*, 4th ed. (New Haven, CT: Yale University Press, 2001), 230.

2. U.S. Department of the Interior, National Park Service, *The National Parks Index* (Washington DC: Government Printing Office, 1995), 22. The battle for the Grand Canyon is extensively covered in Nash, *Wilderness and the American Mind*, 227–37.

3. A classic expression of this assertion is Garrett Hardin, "The Economics of Wilderness," *Natural History* 78 (June–July 1969): 20–27.

4. A brief history of the Grand Canyon Railway may be found in Runte, *Trains of Discovery*, 69–74. The official history of the railway is Al Richmond, *Cowboys, Miners, Presidents and Kings: The Story of the Grand Canyon Railway*, multiple editions (Flagstaff: Grand Canyon Railway, 1989–present).

13 — Future Imperfect

1. A definitive introduction to the philosophy of high-speed rail is Joseph Vranich, *Supertrains: Solutions to America's Transportation Gridlock* (New York: St. Martin's, 1991).

2. A period assessment of the GG1 is Austin C. Lescarboura, "The Miracle of the Electric Locomotive," *Travel* 69 (July 1937): 4–10.

3. An entertaining introduction to the idea of the future is Joseph J. Corn et al., *Yesterday's Tomorrows: Past Visions of the American Future* (Baltimore: Johns Hopkins University Press, 1996).

4. Garrett Hardin, *Exploring New Ethics for Survival: The Voyage of the* Spaceship Beagle (New York: Viking, 1972).

5. James Bryce, "National Parks—The Need of the Future," *The Outlook* 102 (December 14, 1912): 811.

6. Bryce, "National Parks," 811–12.

14 — The Time We Save

1. Rogers E. M. Whitaker, *All Aboard with E. M. Frimbo: World's Greatest Railroad Buff* (New York: Viking, 1974).

15 — Something Real

1. A telling example of this criticism is Joseph Vranich, *End of the Line: The Failure of Amtrak Reform and the Future of America's Passenger Trains* (Washington DC: American Enterprise Institute Press, 2004), 79–85. Says Vranich: "Given how marginal rail travel is to meeting America's travel needs, there is clearly no justification for keeping long-distance routes as part of a 'national passenger rail system' that hasn't existed for decades" (81).

16 — Power and Obligation

1. Timeless expressions of this argument may be found in Vranich, *End of the Line*.

2. The significance of these figures is further discussed in Runte, *Trains of Discovery*, 28–29.

3. Michael P. Malone, *James J. Hill: Empire Builder of the Northwest* (Norman: University of Oklahoma Press, 1996), 199.

4. A listing of worldwide privatization efforts can be found in Vranich, *End of the Line*, 195–202.

5. Rail passenger advocates heard many such comments at "Rail is Real," The National Corridors Initiative Conference, Washington DC, June 26–27, 2000.

17 — Rethinking Europe

1. Eric Julber, "Let's Open Up Our Wilderness Areas," *Reader's Digest* 100 (May 1972): 125–28.

2. Plans for such a railroad had already materialized. See Christopher Swan and Chet Roaman, *YV 88: An Eco-Fiction of Tomorrow* (San Francisco: Sierra Club Books, 1977). See also Runte, "Yosemite Valley Railroad."

3. Rick Steves, *Germany, Austria and Switzerland, 1999* (Santa Fe, NM: John Muir Publications, 1999), 243–44.

Epilogue: The Land Would Ask for Trains

1. Nash, *Wilderness and the American Mind*, 44.

2. An emerging awareness among railroads of the need to rebuild their capacity is revealingly described in Daniel Machalaba, "Making Tracks: Big Railroads Race to Cross U.S., Again," *Wall Street Journal*, December 28, 2004, A–1.

3. Leopold, *A Sand County Almanac*, 224–25.

4. Geyer, "Here, the Pieces of Life Flow Together."

For Further Reading

My notes will direct the reader to the sources of quotations and statistics used in the text. The following will identify the important secondary works that, as they appeared, influenced the nation's thinking—and mine—on the future of passenger rail.

Two recent histories of importance are Richard J. Orsi, *Sunset Limited: The Southern Pacific Railroad and the Development of the West, 1850–1930* (Berkeley: University of California Press, 2005), and Carlos A. Schwantes, *Railroad Signatures across the Pacific Northwest* (Seattle: University of Washington Press, 1993). Both books, as environmental history, confirm that although the western railroads were engines of development, they balanced conquest with the quest for tourism. Environmental themes imbue another book, James E. Vance Jr.'s *The North American Railroad: Its Origin, Evolution, and Geography* (Baltimore: Johns Hopkins University Press, 1995). Like Orsi and Schwantes, Vance adds to our understanding of railroad passengers, especially their perspectives from a train.

The writings of John R. Stilgoe further consider railroads as the creators of a sense of place. In *Metropolitan Corridor: Railroads and the American Scene* (New Haven, CT: Yale University Press, 1983), he notes that not every passenger on America's railroads was attracted by the scenery. Some were bored by it, others even repulsed. Invariably, one's purpose in traveling influences what one sees. Of course, not every passenger gave the landscape rapt attention. The point is that railroads gave passengers the opportunity. And even Stilgoe admits that early observation cars, with open platforms, delighted tourists of every age.

As an object of industrial design, the passenger train has an admirable biographer in Karl R. Zimmermann, CZ: *The Story of the* California Zephyr (Starrucca, PA: Starrucca Valley Publications, 1972). Although other railroads attempted to copy it, the *California Zephyr* remained unique. Inaugurated in 1949 between Chicago and Oakland, it was one of the few trains with a daylight passage directly through the Rocky Mountains. Zimmermann's point is clear: a train built for observation is built for landscape. Five vista-domes, each seating twenty-four, allowed virtually every passenger to relate to landscape. Truly, the train's discontinuance in 1970 was a blow to preservation and to historic preservation as well.

Several sources from the 1960s—when passenger trains went on the chopping block—impressed me then and impress me now. Peter Lyon's *To Hell in a Day Coach: An Exasperated Look at American Railroads* (Philadelphia: J. B. Lippincott, 1968) is exactly what its subtitle claims—exasperated and hard-hitting. When it originally appeared, I was still in college, and hoped its dismal assessment might be reversed. Lyon had no love for railroad executives (better said, railroad moguls), whom he believed had come to haunt the passenger train. Lyon believed the railroads, ignoring the philanthropy of an earlier age, had turned rapacious. Any past credit for being visionary had been compromised in their war against the public. The railroads had brought their worst problems on themselves, now finally to take it out on the passenger train.

In "Why Kill the Passenger Train" *(Journal of Marketing* 28 [January 1964]: 1–6), Stanley Berge informed Lyon and many activists, but not the railroads. Berge's insistence that government regulation was a greater problem than competing cars and airplanes pleased the railroads, but only to a point. They wanted to be rid of regulation, surely, but also to be done with the passenger train. A few railroads agreed with Berge that the Interstate Commerce Commission improperly assessed fixed costs. However, the vast majority, wanting out of the passenger business, were glad to have the ICC's formula. With it they could play the numbers, dumping extra costs on the passenger train.

In marked contrast, another period book, *Megalopolis Unbound: The Supercity and the Transportation of Tomorrow* (New York: Praeger, 1966), looked optimistically to the future. The writer was a politician, after all, someone with more clout than a university economist. The political savvy (and the clout) was from Rhode Island's Senator Claiborne Pell. Elected to Congress in 1962, Pell found a niche advocating high-speed rail. Of course, his constituents would reap the benefits. Rhode Island, lying between Boston and New York, was part of the supercity he was writing about. There, the railroads would have to approve and accept the aid of government. No city of such size and complexity could live on cars alone.

However, where urban congestion had not forced the issue, environmentalists were strangely quiet. A memorable exception was Michael Frome, "Ten Lovely Train Rides," *Woman's Day* (November 1963): 76–77, 134–36. Like the progressives, Frome believed that what was lovely about taking trains was their commitment to a sense of place.

Along the same lines, a wonderful book with an unfortunate title is Rogers E. M. Whitaker, *All Aboard with E. M. Frimbo: World's Greatest Railroad Buff* (New York: Viking, 1974). The title implies the obsessive behavior for which rail fans are renowned. Whitaker's articles, written under a pen name for *The New Yorker*, were so much more. This anthology is hardly just for railroad buffs, focusing equally on Whitaker's love of place. Using the dismissive word "buff" for Whitaker and many other writers has a crippling effect on railroad scholarship and on the revival of the passenger train.

Oliver Jensen's "A Cautionary Tale" (*American Heritage* 20 [December 1968]: 10–15) is another article I read at the time and, again, appreciated instantly for its observation that the passenger train was being attacked by national indifference. Thirty-five years later, railroad abandonment in general became the subject of two books by Joseph P. Schwieterman: *When the Railroad Leaves Town: American Communities in the Age of Rail Line Abandonment—Eastern United States* and *When the Railroad Leaves Town: American Communities in the Age of Rail Line Abandonment—Western United States* (Kirksville, MO: Truman State University Press, 2001 and 2004, respectively). Using a case-study approach, Schwieterman's books are a telling reminder that even as cities and towns suffered from the loss of railroads, so did the American landscape.

Another recent article is Mark Reutter's "The Lost Promise of the American Railroad" (*The Wilson Quarterly* 18 [Winter 1994]: 10–37). With admirable brevity, Reutter lays out the railroads' plight—both cultural and self-inflicted—after World War II. The decline began in the 1930s, he notes, when railroads failed in their own attempts to modernize. His telling example is the *Pioneer Zephyr,* the Burlington Railroad's historic high-speed train. Inaugurated May 26, 1934, the *Zephyr* made the 1,015-mile run between Denver and Chicago in 13 hours, 4 minutes, and 58 seconds, nearly halving the time of conventional trains. By the 1950s, one would have expected trains like the *Pioneer Zephyr* to be commonplace. Reutter links the opposite result to a decline in the industry so precipitous that no technology could possibly save it. Simply, "The business was beyond the therapy of traction power" (35).

Undaunted, Joseph Vranich remains convinced that traction is the answer, if not on conventional railroads, then on new ones built for speed. Such is the theme of *Supertrains: Solutions to America's Transportation Gridlock* (New York: St. Martin's, 1991) and *Derailed: What Went Wrong and What to Do About America's Passenger Trains* (New York: St. Martin's, 1997). Vranich's perspective suffers from his acceptance of the railroads' version of their history, namely, that the public abandoned them. His latest book, *End of the Line: The Failure of Amtrak Reform and the Future of America's Passenger Trains* (Washington DC: American Enterprise Institute Press, 2004), even denies there is a history. Although Amtrak gets an entire chapter, it is but two and a half pages long, to explain a period of thirty-five years. Far more analytical and truly comparative is Anthony Perl, *New Departures: Rethinking Rail Passenger Policy in the Twenty-First Century* (Lexington:

University Press of Kentucky, 2002). As Perl shows, a good part of America's problem is its terminology. Where the passenger train serves the world and excites it, the cultural definitions are favorable to railroads, while ours are not.

In *Railroads Triumphant: The Growth, Rejection, and Rebirth of a Vital American Force* (New York: Oxford University Press, 1992), Albro Martin similarly defines the historical problem narrowly. Overregulation did the railroads in. Peter Lyon's contention that the railroads blatantly manipulated their regulators (*To Hell in a Day Coach*) is generally overlooked, as is the point that the railroads, as public utilities, just might require government oversight. Lyon, as the more critical author, seems closer to the actual history. As soon as the railroads won deregulation, in 1980, they did just as history would have predicted—rushed to form monopolies. How is that good for trade or landscape?

The prior century of competition among the railroads undoubtedly better served the environment, as reflected in the arts. *The Railroad in American Art: Representations of Technological Change* by Susan Danly and Leo Marx (Cambridge, MA: MIT Press, 1988) wonderfully explores the theme. Barbara Novak, *Nature and Culture: American Landscape and Painting, 1825–1875* (New York: Oxford University Press, 1980), has much on railroads too. Clive Irving, in "If You Think This Is Travel, You're Crazy," (*Condé Nast Traveler* [September 1992]: 129), postulates that the problem with railroads is all about abandoning culture, specifically, giving up on the idea of a continent whose aesthetic gift is size.

The best natural histories describe the gift, if hardly mentioning trains. The value of that genre remains inspirational for understanding why technological discipline is needed for landscape. Aldo Leopold's *A Sand County Almanac* (New York: Oxford University Press, 1949) calls for restraint of many kinds, including a love of walking into wilderness rather than relying on motorized access. Edward Abbey, in *Desert Solitaire: A Season in the Wilderness* (New York: Ballantine, 1968), speaks foremost to resignation. People have always failed wilderness, and always will. Perhaps if Abbey and Leopold had included railroads in their larger observations, they would have dared believe the opposite.

Index

About the Author

An internationally acclaimed environmentalist and environmental historian, Alfred Runte came to the subject of railroads while exploring the American land. Born and raised in Binghamton, New York, he began his travels aboard the legendary *Phoebe Snow*, viewing the beautiful and varied American landscape from his window seat. In 1959, following the death of his father, his mother took the family west on a 10,000-mile camping trip, visiting the national parks. Years later, while pursuing his PhD at the University of California, Santa Barbara, he realized that the parks had been formed by railroads. America's identity is the land, and our love for the land was first made possible by the railroads. Truly, *Allies of the Earth* has been a book in the making for more than 50 years.

Now an independent scholar and consultant, Runte still travels widely on behalf of railroads and the environment, most recently to Brazil, where he gave the keynote address at the Fourth Brazilian Congress on Parks and Protected Areas in October 2004. He is also on the editorial board of *Natureza & Conservação,* the environmental journal of Brazil's Fundação O Boticário de Proteção à Natureza. He remains a board member of the Center for the Study of the Environment in Santa Barbara, California, and has served on the boards of the National Parks Conservation Association, National Association of Railroad Passengers, University of Alaska Press, and Susquehanna Conservation Council.

Runte has taught at five colleges and universities and worked on the staff of the Smithsonian Insitution. He has consulted for the National Park Service and the U.S. Forest Service, and spent four summers as a seasonal ranger in Yosemite National Park. Currently, he is an advisor to Ken Burns for a forthcoming PBS series on the national parks, which will air in 2009. He has been a featured guest on *Nightline* (ABC), *The Today Show* (NBC), *Forty-Eight Hours* (CBS), The History Channel, and The Travel Channel. *Allies of the Earth* is his fifth major book.